Miscarriages of Justice
Famous London Cases

TRUE CRIME FROM WHARNCLIFFE

Foul Deeds and Suspicious Deaths Series

Barking, Dagenham & Chadwell Heath
Barnsley
Bath
Bedford
Birmingham
Black Country
Blackburn and Hyndburn
Bolton
Bradford
Brighton
Bristol
Cambridge
Carlisle
Chesterfield
Colchester
Coventry
Croydon
Derby
Dublin
Durham
Ealing
Folkestone and Dover
Grimsby
Guernsey
Guildford
Halifax
Hampstead, Holborn and St Pancras
Huddersfield
Hull

Leeds
Leicester
Lewisham and Deptford
Liverpool
London's East End
London's West End
Manchester
Mansfield
More Foul Deeds Birmingham
More Foul Deeds Chesterfield
More Foul Deeds Wakefield
Newcastle
Newport
Norfolk
Northampton
Nottingham
Oxfordshire
Pontefract and Castleford
Portsmouth
Rotherham
Scunthorpe
Southend-on-Sea
Staffordshire and The Potteries
Stratford and South Warwickshire
Tees
Warwickshire
Wigan
York

OTHER TRUE CRIME BOOKS FROM WHARNCLIFFE

Foul Deeds and Suspicious Deaths Series
A-Z of Yorkshire Murder
Black Barnsley
Brighton Crime and Vice 1800-2000
Durham Executions
Essex Murders
Executions & Hangings in Newcastle and Morpeth
Norfolk Mayhem and Murder

Norwich Murders
Strangeways Hanged
The A-Z of London Murders
Unsolved Murders in Victorian and
Edwardian London
Unsolved Norfolk Murders
Unsolved Yorkshire Murders
Yorkshire's Murderous Women

Please contact us via any of the methods below for more information or a catalogue.

WHARNCLIFFE BOOKS

47 Church Street – Barnsley – South Yorkshire – S70 2AS
Tel: 01226 734555 – 734222 Fax: 01226 – 734438
E-mail: enquiries@pen-and-sword.co.uk
Website: www.wharncliffebooks.co.uk

Miscarriages of Justice

Famous London Cases

John J Eddleston

First published in Great Britain in 2009 by
Wharncliffe Local History
an imprint of
Pen & Sword Books Ltd
47 Church Street
Barnsley
South Yorkshire
S70 2AS

ISBN 978 1 84563 096 6

A CIP catalogue record for this book is available from the British Library.

Printed and bound in the UK by
MPG Books Group

Pen & Sword Books Ltd incorporates the Imprints of
Pen & Sword Aviation, Pen & Sword Family History,
Pen & Sword Maritime, Pen & Sword Military, Wharncliffe Local History,
Pen & Sword Select, Pen & Sword Military Classics, Leo Cooper,
Remember When, Seaforth Publishing and Frontline Publishing

For a complete list of Pen & Sword titles please contact
PEN & SWORD BOOKS LIMITED
47 Church Street, Barnsley, South Yorkshire, S70 2AS, England
E-mail: enquiries@pen-and-sword.co.uk
Website: www.pen-and-sword.co.uk

Contents

Introduction

In the twentieth century a total of 865 people were executed in the United Kingdom. In the years since the abolition of capital punishment just four of those people have received posthumous pardons: Timothy John Evans, Derek William Bentley, Mahmood Hussein Mattan and George Kelly.

It may be that the reader believes that it is acceptable that four innocent men were hanged, out of a total of 865, but when one has researched every single one of those cases, as I have, then the number who may well have been innocent appears to rise. It is my personal opinion that there was either a reasonable doubt, or obvious signs of mental instability – or some other factor that indicates that there should not have been an execution, in over 100 of those cases.

Yet this only covers the cases where someone was actually put to death. If one adds other cases where the death sentence was commuted, or where a life sentence was given after capital punishment had been abolished, then the number rises even further.

This book looks at just nine cases, involving twelve people who were tried for murder. Of those twelve, nine were sentenced to death and eight actually executed. More importantly, five of those twelve have since been pardoned. And these are only cases from London; what of those from the rest of the country?

Read the stories for yourself and decide whether you would really sanction either the execution, or the imprisonment for years, of those whose stories are told in these pages.

Acknowledgements

I would like to thank my partner, Yvonne Eddleston, for her invaluable help in preparing this volume. Not only did she assist with the research but she also proof-read every story before I submitted the manuscript.

I would also wish to thank the staff of the The National Archives at Kew, who always make it a pleasure to visit. In addition, my thanks must go to the British Newspaper Library at Colindale.

Finally I would like to offer my appreciation to my publisher, Wharncliffe Books.

Chapter 1

Louise Josephine Jemima Massett
1899-1900

On Friday 27 October 1899, two ladies alighted from a train at Dalston Junction railway station. Mary Teahan was a governess, living at 46 Walpole Street, Isleworth. Her friend, Margaret Ellen Briggs, lived at Twickenham and both ladies had caught a train from Richmond in Surrey, to Dalston, so that they might attend a lecture in a schoolroom close by. The train had been due to arrive at 6.05pm but was running a little late. As a result, it was close on 6.19pm when Mary and Margaret climbed down onto Platform 3.

The two ladies walked into the ladies' waiting room on that same platform and Margaret waited there whilst Mary went down the passageway which led to the water closets. There were two cubicles inside and Mary Teahan chose to enter the first, but upon trying to gain entry, she found that something behind the door was blocking her way.

The cubicle was far from well lit but in the dim light Mary saw what appeared to be a child's face – but surely that could not be. No, it was most probably another lady who had fallen ill. The matter must be reported at once.

Mary left the water closets area and rejoined her friend, Margaret to whom she mentioned what she had discovered. It was then that they spotted a porter, pushing a barrow along the platform. Joseph John Standing listened closely as Mary Teahan told him that she thought there was a lady who might have fainted or fallen ill inside the first cubicle. Then, perhaps rather surprisingly, having told their story, neither lady waited on the platform. They left the station and continued on their way to their destination.

It was 6.38pm by the time Joseph Standing told Mr Cotteral,

the foreman porter, what the ladies had told him. On Cotteral's instructions, Standing then took the story to the station inspector, David Bundy. It was now approximately 6.40pm.

Bundy informed Standing that he should go to the water closet and check the story for himself. Standing did as he had been instructed and entered the ladies toilets. He walked first to the second cubicle, the one farthest from the entrance and saw nothing untoward. It was then that he gently pushed open the

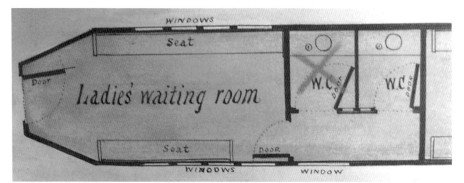

A police drawing of the layout of the toilets on the platform at Dalston Junction Station. The National Archives

Another police artist's drawing of the ladies toilet where Manfred's body was discovered. This drawing was used as an exhibit in Louise's trial. The National Archives

door of the first cubicle and found that there was something on the floor behind the door.

The first thing Standing saw was a dark coloured shawl but then, to his horror, he saw that this shawl partly covered the body of a small child. Without a moment's delay, Standing returned to Mr Bundy and told him what he had seen.

David Bundy now took a lamp and entered the toilets for himself. He saw the body of a small boy. The shawl had been laid loosely over his torso but his head, throat and feet were exposed. Bundy tried to feel for a pulse to see if the boy was still alive, but found none. He did notice that the boy's flesh beneath the shawl was slightly warm to the touch but his extremities were quite cold. Bundy also noticed that the boy's face was smeared with blood and, on the floor, close to his head, was a clinker brick split into two parts, one part being either side of the head. Bundy then ordered that the doctor and the police should be sent for immediately.

Constable James Patman timed his arrival at the station at 6.48pm. The officer did not touch anything at the scene but stood guard until the doctor arrived.

At 6.58pm, Dr James Patrick Fennell arrived in the cubicle to examine the child's body. He made a careful note of the position of the body. The child's head was towards the corridor. His left leg was bent at the knee with the left foot underneath the right thigh. Dr Fennell also felt the child's trunk and found it warm. There was no sign of rigor mortis at this stage. The boy's tongue protruded slightly from his teeth, an indication that suffocation might well be the cause of death though of course that would be determined properly at the post-mortem. At this initial examination, Dr Fennell believed that the boy had been dead for approximately one hour, thus putting the time of death at around 6.00pm.

Reports of the discovery of the boy's body, together with a description, were published in the London newspapers. On the morning of Monday 30 October, one of those reports was seen by a young governess, named Helen Eliza Gentle, who lived at 210 Clyde Road, Tottenham. What she read caused her such great concern that she first went to see her family doctor to ask for his advice. Acting on that advice, Helen then went to the Hackney Mortuary where the child's body lay, and asked if she might see it as she may well be able to provide an identification. Now she was sure, and Helen took her story to the police. The body had been positively identified as that of Manfred Louis Masset, who had been three and a half years old.

Helen Gentle took a good deal of time to tell the police what she knew. She told the officers investigating the case that she lived with her mother and step-father and she had first met Manfred soon after he had been born. Helen had placed an advertisement in the newspaper saying that she was willing to take a child and act as its nurse. It was this which brought Louise Masset to her house in Clyde Road and, as a result of that interview, she took Louise's new-born child, Manfred, who had been born on 24 April 1896, for a payment of £1 17s per month.

Manfred Louis Masset. This photograph was taken on the very day Helen Gentle handed Manfred over to his mother. It was also the day he was murdered. The National Archives

Louise, it seems, was an unmarried mother and could not take care of the boy herself, due to her family not being willing to accept him. Miss Masset taught French and music and was quite able to pay for the child's upkeep however, her sister was willing to act as a guarantor for the money. In fact, that guarantee had never been called upon. Louise had paid the £1 17s regularly, usually in advance, and had visited her son on a fortnightly basis. Over the last few months, those visits had become more frequent with Louise visiting once a week, almost always on a Wednesday. Things had continued in this way until Wednesday 18 October when Mrs Norris, Helen's mother, had received a letter from Louise in which she stated that it was her intention to take the child away. Apparently his father, who lived in France, had expressed a desire to take the boy and Louise had agreed.

Louise had called, as usual, later that same Wednesday and the matter was discussed further. A date for the hand-over was agreed upon and so, on Friday 27 October, Helen had taken the rather tearful child to the bus stop outside the Birdcage public house on Stamford Hill. Here she handed Manfred over to his mother and Helen saw them both get onto a bus bound for London Bridge station. That bus left Stamford Hill at 12.48pm, and that was the last time Helen had seen Manfred alive.

From Helen Gentle, the police were able to obtain Louise Masset's home address of 29 Bethune Road, Stoke Newington. A number of officers, including Sergeant William Burch, Sergeant Richard Nursey and Detective Constable Allen, now kept watch on that address, from around 3.30pm on that Monday afternoon.

The police saw no sign of Louise Masset during that whole afternoon and evening. Early the following morning, a gentleman arrived and soon afterwards, he was seen to leave with Mr Cadisch, the owner of the house. The police followed the two men to London Bridge station where they identified themselves as police officers. Then, acting on what they had been told, Sergeant Burch and Constable Allen accompanied the two men to the home of George Richard Simes at Croydon. There they found a tearful Louise Masset who readily admitted that she had lied to Miss Gentle but added that she was in no way guilty of her son's murder.

Louise explained that she had, for some time, felt that Manfred might not be getting the best education whilst living with Helen Gentle. One day, on one of her regular Wednesday visits to see Manfred, Louise had taken her son to Tottenham Green where she had fallen into conversation with two ladies named Browning. They had made comments on Manfred as he played with a little girl they had with them and the elder of the two ladies mentioned that they were about to open a small school in King's Road, Chelsea. They offered to take Manfred at a fee of £12 per annum and, after some thought, Louise had agreed.

It was now that Louise saw the opportunity to take advantage of this situation. Her own mother lived next door to Louise, at 31 Bethune Road and she had a lodger, a young Frenchman named Eudor Lucas. Louise and Eudor had grown rather close and it was time to take their relationship to the next step. Louise contacted Eudor and invited him to a weekend trip to Brighton. Eudor agreed but said that due to work commitments, he would only be able to travel down on the Saturday. The plan was simple. Louise would pick Manfred up from Helen Gentle, travel to London Bridge station, hand the boy and the money over to the Brownings and then travel on to Brighton. The next day, Eudor would arrive and they would spend a pleasant couple of days together before going back to London on the Sunday evening. As for Helen Gentle and indeed Louise's own family, she would tell them that Manfred was going to his father in France. After all, they need not know that she had now started a full relationship with young Eudor.

The police listened patiently to this story but felt that they had enough evidence to arrest Louise and charge her with the murder of her son. After a number of appearances before the magistrates, Louise was sent for trial. That trial opened at the Old Bailey on 13 December 1899, before Mr Justice Bruce. The Crown's case was led by Mr Charles Matthews, who was assisted by Mr Richard D Muir. Louise's defence lay in the hands of Lord Coleridge and Mr Arthur Hutton. The proceedings would last until 18 December.

The first important witness was Helen Gentle. She confirmed the details she had given to the police when she had first identified

Manfred's body. Helen had had charge of Manfred since he was some three weeks old and he had stayed at Clyde Road ever since. In fact, the only time Manfred had been separated from Helen was when he had entered the hospital for a circumcision operation.

Helen was able to confirm that Louise seemed to be very fond of her son, a feeling that Manfred reciprocated. The original visits had been once a fortnight but, from about eighteen months ago when Louise had moved to 29 Bethune Road to live with her married sister, the visits had become weekly.

On Wednesday 4 October, Louise had come to visit as usual and had taken Manfred out. The same occurred the following week, on Wednesday 11 October. On that occasion, Helen had met Louise and Manfred later, in Seven Sisters Road, and all three of them had gone to Tottenham Green, arriving there at about 3.30pm and staying until around 5.00pm.

It was on that same 11 October that Manfred appeared to be rather ill. Louise had remarked that he looked rather pale and Helen agreed that he did. He seemed lethargic and tired so Louise carried him back to Clyde Road, where she stayed until some time between 6.00pm and 7.00pm. After Louise had left, Manfred grew sicker and came out in a rash, so the doctor was sent for. He prescribed a tonic, which seemed to make the boy better. Louise had been so concerned that she returned to Helen Gentle's house later that evening and spent the night there.

Louise had promised that because Manfred had been ill she would make a second visit that week, on Friday 13 October. In the event she did not keep that promise and her next visit took place on Wednesday 18 October, the same day that Helen's mother, Mrs Norris, received the letter stating that Manfred was to be sent to his father in France.

When Louise paid her usual visit on the 18th, arrangements were made to hand Manfred over. The original plan, suggested by Helen herself, was that the exchange should take place at London Bridge station. Louise had said that she intended taking Manfred to Newhaven first, and would then sail to France the following day. Later, Helen's mother pointed out that the further she travelled with the boy, the more distressed he might become at the eventual parting. For that reason, on Louise's next visit, 25 October, the arrangements were altered and the exchange was now to take place at the Birdcage public house from where the buses for London Bridge could be caught.

Two days later, on Friday 27 October, Helen took Manfred and two brown paper parcels to Stamford Hill. One of the parcels contained some of the child's clothing, which Louise had specifically asked for. The other contained Manfred's favourite toys, including a small set of scales, which he often used to measure out sugar or currants. Manfred was wearing a little sailor suit at the time and before she handed him over, Helen had his picture taken, as a memento.

Helen and Manfred arrived at the Birdcage first but only had to wait a few minutes before Louise appeared. Manfred was handed over, along with the two parcels and Helen then saw Louise and her son get onto the omnibus. Before the bus left, Helen asked Louise if she would give her a written reference and Louise said that she would be happy to do so and would post the letter from Sussex before she sailed for France.

By now, the police knew, from Louise's own statement, that she had actually travelled to Brighton, where she had stayed from Friday 27 October until Sunday 29 October. On Saturday 28

The ticket added to the parcel of clothing found at Brighton station.
The National Archives

October, a parcel had been found at Brighton station. That parcel had been sent on to London as lost property and there it was opened and found to contain some items of children's clothing. Helen Gentle now identified that clothing as belonging to Manfred and items he had been wearing when she handed him over to his mother. Further, the clothing had still been wrapped in brown paper and when that was examined it was seen that it had been torn from a larger sheet. The remains of that sheet were still at Clyde Road and the police were able to compare the tears. The paper matched exactly. There could be no doubt that the parcel of clothing did contain items that had belonged to Manfred. As if that were not enough, the toy scales had been left in the hotel room in Brighton and Helen was able to positively identify them too.

The next witness was Leonie Cadisch, Louise's sister. Leonie confirmed that she lived with her husband Richard at 29 Bethune Road. She went on to tell the court that Louise had been thirty-six years old last June and had lived next door, at number 31, with their mother, until just before Manfred had been born in April 1896. It had been Leonie who had guaranteed the payment of £1 17s to Helen Gentle, but she had never been called upon to pay it. Louise earned quite enough money as a teacher and governess and had always paid the account herself.

Louise had first mentioned the idea of taking Manfred away from Miss Gentle in February of 1899. She had said that she thought it would be better for the child's education but the matter was then dropped for some time and only mentioned again in October. On the 18th of that month, Louise had said that she was going to send Manfred to a relative of his father's in France. About a week later Louise said that the arrangements had been made and she would be taking Manfred to Newhaven by the 2.30pm train. Leonie had then seen her sister at 12.30pm on Friday 27 October when she was getting ready to go out.

The next time Leonie had seen Louise was at 9.00pm the following Sunday, 29 October. She was very tired and went straight to bed. The following morning, Leonie had asked Louise about the trip and enquired if Manfred had been troublesome in any way. Louise replied that he had cried a little, especially at London Bridge.

Later that same day, at around 1.30pm, Louise had gone out to one of her regular teaching jobs at West Hampstead. Leonie had expected her home at around 8.00pm but she did not return that night. Finally, Leonie was able to say that she had never seen Louise with any black shawl, let alone the one found wrapped around Manfred's body at Dalston Junction.

The prosecution now turned to an examination of that shawl and the next two witnesses gave evidence on it. Maud Clifford was an assistant at McIlroy's Drapers of 161 High Street, Stoke Newington. She recalled selling the shawl on 24 October and believed that Louise Masset was the woman she had sold it to. On 4 November, she had attended an identification parade and picked out Louise as the customer. However, she was unable to swear positively that she was the woman and Maud had to admit that the shop was a very busy one with as many as twenty assistants serving at one time.

Ernest Hoplin Mooney was the manager at McIlroy's and he testified that he had purchased a batch of three black shawls from the manufacturer, Rylands and Son, wholesaler on either 16 October or possibly the 17th. Only one had been sold since and the one found at Dalston Junction was identical to the two remaining in stock. Mooney described the pattern as rather striking but admitted that many other shops sold identical items.

It was now time to turn to Louise's journey with Manfred on the day he met his death. The next witness, Thomas Bonner, was the conductor of the omnibus, which left the Birdcage at 12.48pm on 27 October. He remembered a woman and child travelling together to London Bridge station. The child was certainly Manfred because Bonner remembered his rather distinctive sailor hat, and the fact that the boy was crying. However, he was unable to confirm that Louise had been the woman with him, though he could say that she had a brown paper parcel with her. The bus had arrived at London Bridge at 1.35pm.

The next sighting of Louise with Manfred had been made by Georgina Worley, the waiting room attendant at London Bridge station. Georgina worked in the first-class waiting room, close to the parcels office, on the south side of the station. At around 1.45pm a lady came into the room, with a little boy. From the description of what the boy was wearing, this was certainly Louise and Manfred, though Georgina had failed to pick Louise out at a later identification parade.

Georgina saw Louise put Manfred down on one of the settees and then sit next to him. To make conversation, Georgina told Louise that she looked rather tired and asked if she were travelling by train. Louise had replied: 'No, I am waiting for someone.' At 2.30pm Georgina left the waiting room and by the time she returned ten minutes later, Louise and Manfred had gone.

Where Louise had gone could be described by an attendant in another waiting room. Ellen Rees, who lived in Ruel Road, Tottenham, had come on duty at 2.30pm and at 2.40pm, she saw a woman and little boy come into her waiting room. Ellen noticed that the boy didn't appear to want to be with the woman and was crying a little. Ellen asked him what he was grizzling about and the woman replied that he was missing his nurse. At that point, the woman said that she might be able to settle him by buying him a cake and Ellen observed that he was a fine little boy and asked how old he was.

That this couple were Louise and Manfred is beyond doubt, for the woman replied that the child would be four next April. Very soon afterwards Louise left the waiting room, ostensibly to go to the refreshment room to purchase the cake she had mentioned.

Thus far, the testimony of Ellen Rees had not damaged Louise Massett's case in any way. Louise had confirmed that she was at London Bridge station with her son but claimed that she had handed him over to the Brownings soon afterwards and then caught the four o'clock train to Brighton. Unfortunately however, Ellen Rees had more evidence to give.

According to Ellen's testimony, she had seen Louise again that day, but by then she was alone. It was around 6.54pm when Louise entered that same waiting room and asked for some water so that she could wash. Ellen poured some water into the middle sink in the lavatory area and saw Louise wash her hands. As the

water was being poured, Louise asked what time the next train to
Brighton was and Ellen told her it was at twenty past. A few
minutes later, Louise asked for a clothes brush and whilst she was
brushing herself down, Ellen pointed out that it was quarter past
seven. Ellen saw Louise leave the waiting room at about 7.18pm.
Almost one month later, on 24 November, Ellen had attended an
identity parade and had picked out Louise as the woman she had
seen twice on 27 October.

The time came for the young man Louise had been involved
with, Eudor Lucas, to tell his story. The prosecution case was that
Louise had seen the possibility of a long term relationship with
Eudor, possibly even marriage, but Manfred had been in the way
and that was why she had killed him. Eudor, however, denied that
this could be the case.

Eudor began by saying that he now lived in France but at the
time of Manfred's death, had lived at 31 Bethune Road with
Louise's mother. He was nineteen years of age and first got to
know Louise when she first moved in with her sister at number
29.

At whitsuntide 1899, Eudor, Louise and another couple had
visited Brighton and all four had stayed at Findlay's Hotel at 36
Queen's Road. During that trip, he and Louise had become more
friendly, though nothing improper had taken place between them.

After their return to London they began to walk out together,
despite the fifteen year age difference. They wrote letters to each
other and they used to meet in secret at Loudon Road station.
They would spend some time together before catching the train
to Dalston Junction, the nearest station to Bethune Road, in order
to return home. Louise's family knew nothing of the blossoming
relationship.

At the beginning of September, Louise told Eudor that she had
an illegitimate child, a son, and that he lived with a nurse. Eudor
thanked Louise for being honest with him but said he did not
wish to know any more about the child.

Towards the end of October, Eudor made an appointment to
meet Louise at Liverpool Street station. It was then that she told
him of her intention to go to Brighton the following Friday,

adding that she intended travelling by the 4.00pm train. It was Eudor who said he would like to go with her and said that he would come down on the Saturday. Arrangements were made to stay at the same hotel, *Findlay's,* and Louise said that she would book two rooms in the name of Brooks. She would tell the staff that she expected her brother to come down on the Saturday and would ask for adjacent rooms.

On the Friday, Eudor wrote to 'Miss Brooks' care of *Findlay's Hotel* to confirm the time of his arrival the next day. On Saturday 28 October, he caught the 2.00pm train and arrived at Brighton at 3.20pm. Louise met him at the station and they walked to the hotel together. That night, they slept together for the first time.

On Sunday evening they caught a train back to London Bridge and parted, some sixty yards from Louise's front door, at about 9.00pm. Finally, Eudor confirmed that they had never discussed marriage in any way and there was no such understanding between them.

The testimony of Ellen Rees had left Louise with a problem. She claimed to have caught the 4.00pm train to Brighton but according to Ellen's testimony, she had actually caught a train, which left at 7.22pm, giving her plenty of time to return to Dalston Junction and murder her son. Witnesses were now called who seemed to confirm Ellen Rees' account.

Alice Riall was a chambermaid at *Findlay's Hotel*. She told the court that Louise had arrived at the hotel at 9.45pm on Friday 27 October. She stayed in room 11 and the following day her 'brother' arrived, and occupied room 10. Alice was also able to say that when she had first arrived, Louise had had a rolled up parcel with her.

John Findlay was the owner of the hotel on Queen's Road. He confirmed the time of Louise's arrival as 9.45pm and said she had two parcels with her. The following Wednesday, John had found a pair of toy scales in a drawer in room 11.

The next witness was Ann Skeats, an assistant at the ladies waiting room at Brighton station. She testified that at about 3.30pm on Saturday 28 October, she had found a brown paper parcel in a cupboard in the waiting room. She kept hold of the parcel until 5.40pm, in case someone should come to claim it, after which she handed it to the cloak room porter.

That porter was Henry Court. He kept the parcel until Monday 30 October, when he opened it and found that it contained items of clothing for a child. The next day he sent the parcel on to the Lost Property Office at London Bridge. The parcel was duly received by William James Brown who then handed it over to Sergeant Richard Nursey of the police, on 1 November.

Sergeant Nursey was the next witness. He confirmed that the parcel contained a serge frock and a small blue coat, both of which had subsequently been identified by Helen Gentle. It had been Nursey who also matched the two pieces of brown paper thus proving that the items had indeed belonged to Manfred Masset.

Sergeant Nursey had also done some timings on possible journeys between Dalston Junction and London Bridge. Travelling by train and bus, he had made the journey twice. Once it had taken him twenty-three minutes. On the other occasion it had taken him twenty-five.

The next couple of witnesses were both brothers-in-law of Louise. Richard Cadisch was married to Leonie and he had been home at 29 Bethune Road when Louise returned from Brighton. She seemed perfectly natural and her behaviour was no different. At around 2.00am on the morning of 31 October, George Simes had come to his house and told him that Louise was at his house in Croydon and was quite distraught. She had seen reports that a child had been found dead at Dalston and was sure it was Manfred. Later that morning, Richard and George had left to go to Croydon but on the way they were stopped by two policemen who then accompanied them.

George Richard Simes was married to Louise's other sister and they lived at New Streatham Road, Croydon. At around 11.00pm on Monday 30 October, a rather hysterical Louise called at his house. She told him that she believed she was being hunted for murder but swore that she hadn't done it. She went on to say that she had seen a newspaper report of the child found at Dalston and was sure that it was Manfred. She went on to tell him the story she had told of sending the boy to France and admitted it was a lie. She had actually handed him over to two ladies at London Bridge and then gone on to Brighton where she had spent the weekend with Eudor Lucas. Having listened to this story, George then went to Bethune Road and told Richard Cadisch what had taken place.

The address Louise claimed had been given to her by the to Browning ladies was 45 King's Road, Chelsea. Henry Willis was now called. He lived at that address and ran a dairy from it. He had never operated a school, and did not know anyone of the name Browning.

The next two witnesses were both railway guards and they had travelled on the two Brighton trains on 27 October. William Bowers travelled on the 4.00pm train and confirmed that it left one minute late and arrived in Brighton at 5.19pm. John Whittle was the guard on the 7.22pm train, which also left one minute late, at 7.23pm. It arrived in Brighton at 9.18pm.

There were now just four more important witnesses to hear. The first of these was Inspector Frederick Forth who had had charge of the case. Almost from the moment she had been arrested, Louise had asked to see the body of her son. Permission was refused until after the coroner's hearing on 2 November, when she was finally taken to the mortuary to see him. Upon seeing Manfred she broke down and cried; 'Oh my child, my poor boy.'

A clinker brick had been found near the child's head and Inspector Forth had travelled to 29 Bethune Road and picked up similar bricks from a rockery in the garden. There were also similar bricks in the front garden, forming a sort of border. The inspector had also made the journey from Dalston Junction to London Bridge and it had taken him exactly half an hour.

The last three witnesses all gave medical evidence. Dr James Patrick Fennell had examined the body in situ and later performed the post-mortem. He confirmed that the child had been suffocated, possibly by the placing of a hand over the airways, and also that Manfred had received a blow to the head. The clinker brick could have inflicted the injuries he observed. Originally he had said that he believed the child had been dead for about one hour but now expanded on this saying that it could have been at any time from one to four hours maximum.

Dr Charles Howard Jackson was the divisional police surgeon and he had assisted Dr Fennell at the post-mortem. He agreed with his colleague's findings but disagreed with the estimate as to the time of death. According to Dr Jackson, the child could have been dead as long as eight hours with four a likely minimum.

Dr Thomas Bond was a consulting surgeon at the Westminster Hospital. He had merely studied the various depositions in the case and gave the opinion that death could have occurred within one to four hours.

The time came for Louise to give her story. She told of the meetings with the Brownings and confirmed that they were supposed to take Manfred from her at 2.00pm at London Bridge station. They had waited but when the ladies hadn't appeared by 2.30pm, Louise thought she might have got the wrong waiting room so went to the other one. She left that room at 3.00pm but did not see the Brownings until 3.55pm, just before the 4.00pm train for Brighton was due to leave.

Manfred and the £12 were handed over, along with the parcel of clothing. Louise asked for a receipt and the ladies said they had no paper and would go to the refreshment room to get some. Louise waited a few more minutes but then couldn't wait any longer. She caught the 4.00pm train to Brighton and after arriving on the coast, deposited her bag in the left luggage office. She had thought about taking a walk along the along the pier but it was somewhat damp so she called in at Mutton's restaurant in King's Road where she had something to eat before walking to the shops in west Brighton. She then returned to the station, collected her bag and walked back to *Findlay's Hotel*. She ended by saying that she was not responsible for Manfred's death.

The jury retired to consider their verdict and after an absence of thirty minutes, returned to announce that Louise was guilty as charged, whereupon she was sentenced to death. There was to be no reprieve and on Tuesday 9 January 1900, Louise Masset became the very first person to be executed in the twentieth century, when she was hanged at Newgate prison, by James Billington and William Warbrick.

Was Louise Masset guilty of the murder of her son? Let us look at the most damning parts of the prosecution case. First, there is

Newgate prison where Louise Masset was executed. Author's collection

the motive, that Louise saw Manfred as either an encumbrance to her new relationship with Eudor Lucas, or possibly that he was a financial burden she could no longer afford. In fact, one piece of information effectively negates both of those motives.

During the period between Louise's arrest and her trial Mr Arthur Newton, acting for the defence, had travelled to France to interview Manfred's father. Louise had never told anyone who this man was and at the time he was only identified as Maurice. During his interview with Mr Newton, Maurice confirmed that there had been a regular correspondence between him and Louise from 29 December 1895 up to late 1899. In those letters, Louise had spoken in the most loving of terms for both Manfred and Maurice and there was, perhaps, a hope that one day she and Maurice would be together.

Suddenly, Maurice stopped writing so, on 30 September, Louise sent him a letter asking why she had not heard from him. On Wednesday 4 October, he finally replied to say that he had found another woman to love. She replied that same day, saying that she was very hurt that he had found another and asked Maurice to consider paying a sum of £12 per year, for Manfred's upkeep and education until he reached the age of fifteen.

This is a very important letter. It must be remembered that Louise had first suggested the idea of moving Manfred away from

Helen Gentle's care as early as February 1899. She claimed that she had met the Brownings on 4 October and now, the mention of the sum of £12 fits in perfectly with that story. In addition, her disappointment with Maurice for falling in love with someone else, only manifests itself on that same day. How natural then, that freed from any hope now of ever returning to Manfred's father, she suddenly decides to move the friendship with Eudor Lucas to a new level and suggests a weekend in Brighton together. Added to this, there had been no change in Louise's finances. She had been able to afford Helen Gentle's fees for more than three years and her circumstances had not changed in October 1899. In short, there was no evidence that Louise saw a long-term future with Eudor Lucas or that she had financial concerns. There was simply no motive for her to murder the son she had only ever expressed love for.

The next damaging testimony came from Maud Clifford and Ernest Mooney who both seemed to indicate that the shawl found on Manfred's body had come from their shop and had been purchased by Louise. That identification was not positive and Maud admitted that she could remember no other specific customer from that day. Further, many witnesses including Helen Gentle, Thomas Bonner, Georgina Worley, and Ellen Rees had all given at least partial descriptions of Louise and whilst many had mentioned her black clothing, none had mentioned that she was wearing any kind of shawl.

Next we come to the testimony of Ellen Rees, possibly the most damaging of the prosecution witnesses. Ellen could recall no other lady she had seen on Friday 27 October or any other date around that time, yet apparently she remembered Louise clearly. She admitted in court that perhaps a hundred ladies would pass through her waiting room on an average day, but it seemed that Louise was the only one she could remember. Added to that, she had seen an artist's impression of Louise and read a full description, before she attended the identity parade.

Next we come to Louise's arrival at *Findlay's Hotel*. She claimed that she had spent part of the unaccounted for time in Mutton's restaurant. During the trial, Henry James Streeter had come forward and presented himself to the defence. Henry was a waiter at Mutton's which was situated at 81-84 King's Road in Brighton and he recalled Friday 27 October as it had been rather wet and consequently he had served only two customers all day. One was a man but the other was a woman who was dressed all in black. She had entered the restaurant at around 6.00pm and stayed for forty-five minutes. Both Henry and Mr Mutton, the proprietor, were positive that they could identify the woman if they saw her again.

If Henry Streeter and Mr Mutton had sworn that Louise was that customer then she was in Brighton long before 7.00pm and could not have caught the 7.22pm train as Ellen Rees had stated. Unfortunately, the defence did not see fit to call either witness or arrange for them to attend an identity parade. Only after Louise had been found guilty and sentenced to death were efforts made to use this possible evidence. Louise was asked what she had had to eat at Mutton's and in two statements she gave slightly different replies. In one she said she had eaten two slices of hot meat with gravy and vegetables, with bread and butter and either ale or beer which came to a total of 2s 6d. In the other she omitted the bread and butter and said that she thought she had paid 1s 9d. Neither version agreed with the books at the restaurant, which showed that the female customer had eaten just bread and butter with a pot of tea. It must be remembered, however, that Louise was trying to recall a meal she had eaten some three months before under the duress of having a death sentence over her.

Next we turn to the evidence of the clothing found at Brighton. There can be no doubt that the paper they were wrapped in had come from Helen Gentle's house and that the items found had belonged to Manfred. Of equal significance, however, is what wasn't found.

Only two items were found in the parcel at Brighton station. The first of these was a navy blue serge frock, which had had white lace on the cuffs and around the collar together with a band around the waist. The lace had been torn from the collar and cuffs and the waist-band had been removed. The other item was a blue cloth coat which had had brass anchor buttons with two fawn capes attached. Again it had a lace collar and cuffs. The collar and cuffs had been removed, as had the buttons.

What the court failed to notice is that the parcel of clothing handed over, and the other items worn by Manfred on the day he died, numbered more than a dozen and included two petticoats, brown shoes, gaiters and a white ribbon tie. None of these items were ever found. Are we to believe that Louise was careful enough to destroy all trace of these items and yet foolish enough to leave just two in a parcel where it was certain to be found? Is it not more likely that someone else planted those two items in order to incriminate Louise? After all, the Brownings, if they existed, had been told by Louise that she intended to catch the Brighton train when they finally made their appearance at London Bridge.

Then there were other witnesses who came forward, but were never called to appear at the trial. On 27 October, David Taylor was on an omnibus at the corner of Bishopsgate and Cornhill. He saw two women, with a child, a little boy, who appeared to be distressed.

John Hughes-Ellis was also on an omnibus, which stopped at London Bridge, and he too saw two women with a little boy who seemed unwilling to be with them. Both of these gentlemen gave times before 4.00pm, when Louise said she had handed the boy over but both also admitted that they were only guessing at the times and it may well have been later.

We must then consider the actual time of death. Three medical opinions put it at somewhere between one and eight hours before Manfred's body was discovered. Much was made of the coldness of the lavatory, the draught there, the fact that Manfred's torso was warm when he was found but one very important fact was never considered. When the various railway employees had given their evidence they all reported that as many as one hundred trains a day called at Dalston Junction. At around 6.00pm there might be as many as twenty per hour with many people alighting from those trains. Are we expected to believe that at such a busy station no one entered that ladies lavatory, for as long as eight hours, until Mary Teahan entered it at around 6.20pm? The very number of people using that station would imply that the body would be discovered relatively quickly. It is this, plus the testimony of Dr Fennell, which makes it much more probable that one hour before discovery is the closest time of death. Manfred, therefore, was murdered at around 6.00pm, just twenty minutes before his body was discovered.

If Louise was the killer then we have to assume that Ellen Rees might well have been correct when she said she saw the accused for a second time at 6.54pm. The various police timings of the journey from Dalston Junction to London Bridge put the time at anything from twenty-three to thirty minutes. If we assume a mean time of around twenty-five minutes then the latest time that Louise could have killed Manfred was twenty-five minutes before 6.54pm or around 6.29pm and the earliest, according to the medical evidence, was around 6.00pm. The body was found at 6.20pm, so that narrows the window of time down to just nine minutes or so. Yet this too misses one important point.

Louise arrived at London Bridge station on Thomas Bonner's omnibus at 1.35pm. She was last seen, during this period, at a few minutes after 2.40pm, by the ever present Ellen Rees. If the journey back to Dalston Junction only took a half hour or so, then Louise could have been back there with her son by 3.10pm. Yet, all the evidence seems to indicate a time of death around 6.00pm. What was she doing for that unaccounted for three hours or so?

The only solution that fits the prosecution case is that Louise first thought of killing Manfred as early as February 1899. Otherwise, why would she have suggested to her sister that he should be taken from Helen Gentle. She then forgot the idea for the best part of a year. Despite holding out hope of a reconciliation with Maurice, the boy's father, she embarked on a relationship with a man half her age, hoping that he would perhaps marry her and in that hope, decided to remove a possible obstacle: her son.

On the day she murdered her son she travelled to London Bridge station where she was seen by a number of witnesses. She then took three and a half hours to make a half hour journey back to the railway station closest to her home where she killed the boy she loved by striking him with a brick, smothering him and then stripping him naked. She took the boy's clothes with her but left a shawl she had just purchased, draped over his body.

She travelled back to London Bridge, possibly disposing of the clothing somewhere along the way but being careful to keep two of the most identifiable items, which she took with her to Brighton. The following day, having mutilated these two items, she left them at Brighton station wrapped in the same piece of paper Helen Gentle had given her. Then, finally, she came up with the story of two women named Browning to whom she had given Manfred and the coincidental sum of £12 she had recently mentioned in a letter to Maurice.

Surely it is just as likely that the Browning ladies did exist and that they did offer to take Manfred for £12. Louise then wrote to Maurice, asking for that sum so that she could maintain the school position without troubling her own finances. These two ladies knew all about Louise; she had given them all they needed to know during their two conversations at Tottenham Green. They killed Manfred, in Louise's local station. They travelled to Brighton the next day and deposited two items of clothing in the brown paper Louise had handed to them.

That may sound like supposition but it makes as much sense as the alternative. Added to that there is the letter posted to Louise at Newgate prison, after she had been tried and sentenced to death. It was dated 26 December and read:

> *The women of Chelsea must keep out of sight but they are not anxious to hang you. If the porter (a porter) at Dalston Junction would speak he could tell who he saw at 4.45 there. Anyhow, put this in your lawyer's hands – it may save you.*

The letter was not passed on by the authorities, and the defence were never told of its existence. It may, of course, have been a hoax, but it may also add weight to that alternative scenario.

Remember that one does not have to prove innocence. One only has to prove that there is a reasonable doubt. In the case of Louise Masset, by all accounts a loving mother, who had no motive to murder the son she adored, that reasonable doubt is plain to see.

Chapter 2

Arthur Devereux
1905

It was almost three weeks since Ellen Gregory had seen her daughter, Beatrice, or her grandchildren.

Beatrice had been married to Arthur Devereux since 2 November 1898. Their first child, Stanley, had been born just over nine months later, on 24 August 1899. Then, on 5 April 1903, the couple had had twin boys: Laurence Rowland and Evelyn Lancelot. Now, it was Tuesday 14 February 1905, and

Beatrice Devereux with her eldest child, Stanley, when he was still a baby. The National Archives

1898.	Marriage solemnized at *Trinity Church* in the *Parish* of *Paddington* in the County of *London*							
No.	When Married.	Name and Surname.	Age.	Condition.	Rank or Profession.	Residence at the time of Marriage.	Father's Name and Surname.	Rank or Profession of Father.
245	*Second November 1898*	*Arthur Devereux*	27	*Bachelor*	*Chemist & Druggist*	*Essex House Malvern Link*	*Arthur James Devereux*	*Chemist & Dru...*
		Beatrice Ellen Maud Gregory	24	*Spinster*	*Professor of Music*	*16 Eastbourne Terrace*	*Charles Gregory*	*Solicitor*

Married in the *said Church* according to the Rites and Ceremonies of the Established Church, *after Banns, by me, G. L. Harding*

| This Marriage was solemnized between us, | *Arthur Devereux* | in the presence of us. | *Hilda May Gregory* |
| | *Beatrice Ellen Maud Gregory* | | *Ellen Gregory* |

I Certify, that the foregoing is a true Extract from the Register of Marriages belonging to *Trinity Church* in the Parish of *Paddington*. Witness my hand this *second* day of *November* 1898 *G. L. Hardi...*

* Note.—Strike out that which does not apply.

Designation *Cura...*

Devereux's marriage certificate. The National Archives

Ellen had been working away from home for a time. She had written to Beatrice but, rather surprisingly, had not had the common courtesy of a reply. It was most unlike her daughter to simply ignore her like this.

Beatrice and Ellen had last met on Saturday 28 January when Beatrice had visited her mother at her home, 85 Minet Avenue. From there, the two ladies went shopping together and, after about an hour and a half, they parted company at around

The house at 60 Milton Avenue, where Arthur Devereux was alleged to have murdered his wife and two children. The National Archives

The rear of the house at 60 Milton Avenue. Note the two children in the window of the house next door, curious to know what the police photographer is doing. The National Archives

11.00pm, with Beatrice then returning to her own home, at 60 Milton Avenue, Harlesden. Now, however, Ellen Gregory was unable to get any reply to her knocking at that address. Surely Beatrice hadn't gone out at this time of day?

Ellen decided to enquire next door so called at number 58, the home of Edward Alfred Wells and his wife Sarah. It was Sarah Wells whom Ellen spoke to and what she heard came as a complete surprise. Apparently, the Devereuxs were no longer living next door. Sarah told Ellen that she had seen a van at the front door, exactly one week before, on 7 February. The van was loaded up with boxes and some items of furniture and Arthur Devereux and his son Stanley went off with it. Sarah was, however, able to give Ellen one more piece of information. The van bore the name of Bannister on the side.

It was a simple matter for Ellen Gregory to trace the company to their offices in Kensal Rise, which she visited a few days later. By speaking to employees of Bannisters, Ellen was able to discover that the items moved on 7 February had been taken to an address at 92 Harrow Road. All, that is, except for one large tin trunk, which had been left in storage.

The next port of call, the following week, was 92 Harrow Road. Here Ellen spoke to the owner of the house, one John Tabboth. He confirmed that he had advertised a part of his house, as a bedsitter, in early February. On 6 February Mr Devereux had called to view it and agreed a rent of five shillings per week. There was, however, one problem. Mr Devereux explained that he had a son who was almost five years old. The bedsitter only had one bed and he would need another for his son, Stanley. Mr Tabboth said that this would not be a problem. He put another single bed into the rooms and Arthur and Stanley moved in the next day.

Ellen's first thought now was what had happened to Beatrice and the twins. She asked Mr Tabboth if Arthur had mentioned them and he confirmed that he had been told that they were away in the country as Beatrice was recovering from an illness. This did not ring true, for Ellen had seen that Beatrice was perfectly healthy when they had last met and, of course, that would not explain why there had been no letter or telegram from her. John Tabboth had one other piece of information to impart. On 20 February, Devereux had moved on yet again, saying that he had a new job in Coventry. Stanley had been left behind with Mr Tabboth but on 25 March, after hearing from Devereux, Tabboth had put Stanley on a train so that he could go to his father in the Midlands.

Ellen Gregory now had a good deal of information. She knew that Arthur and Stanley had moved alone to Harrow Road, that there had been no sign of Beatrice or the twins, and that Arthur and Stanley were now in Coventry. Indeed, she even had the address of Arthur Devereux's new employer since he had written to Mr Tabboth on a letterhead. It was time to take her concerns to the police.

The police made their own enquiries and, as a result, it was not until the morning of Thursday 13 April that they went to Bannister's offices to examine the contents of the tin trunk. The trunk was securely padlocked, had straps around it, and was sealed with red wax so that it was airtight, presumably to protect

The trunk after it had been opened. The bodies can clearly be seen.
The National Archives

the contents. After all, when it was deposited, Devereux had said that it contained books and chemicals. The locks were forced and the lid of the trunk lifted. Inside, officers found a layer of wooden planks, carefully fitted together and sealed with glue, more wax and a white powder which tests would later show was Boric Acid. The planks were removed to reveal a quilt and a tablecloth and when they were taken out, the real content were finally revealed; the bodies of Beatrice Devereux and her twin sons.

The letters written by Devereux to Mr Tabboth bore the address of 156 Spon Street, Coventry. That address was a chemist's shop, belonging to Mr Bird, and it was there, on the same evening that the three bodies had been found, that Devereux was arrested on suspicion of murder. He was escorted back to London and somewhere on that journey made the comment: 'My conscience is perfectly clear as to their deaths but I was wrong in concealing the bodies.'

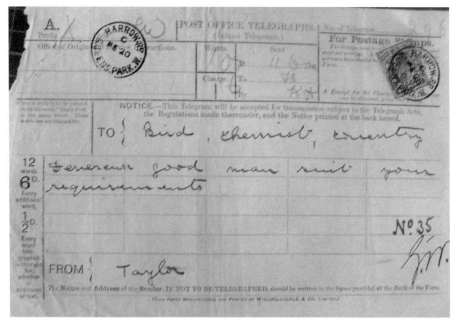

The reference Mr Bird received for Devereux. The National Archives

Arthur Devereux faced his trial at the Old Bailey on 26 July, before Mr Justice Ridley. Throughout the four days the proceedings lasted, the prisoner was defended by Mr George Elliott, Mr Arthur Hutton and Mr Cecil Fitch. The case for the prosecution was led by Mr Charles Matthews who was assisted by Mr Bodkin.

Devereux pleaded not guilty to murder. His story was simple; he had come home one day to find his wife and twin sons dead. It was obvious that she had murdered the boys and then taken her own life. In a panic, he had merely hidden the bodies. It was up to the prosecution to show that in fact, it was Devereux who had killed all three members of his family and then invented this story to save himself.

Ellen Gregory was quite scathing in her evidence. She told the court that whilst Devereux had doted on Stanley, his eldest son, he had been disappointed with the twins. This was partly because there were two extra mouths to feed, but another factor was that the two boys were not in perfect health. Both had rickets, which meant that they could not walk unaided, or feed themselves. Ellen also confirmed that Beatrice had loved all her children equally and was a good and dutiful mother.

That Arthur Devereux had not had much time for his twins seemed to be partly contradicted by the evidence of James Maldon. James lived at 23 Malvern Road, West Kilburn, and he stated that the Devereux family had lived with him, as lodgers, from August 1904 to 31 December of that same year. He had not seen a great deal of Arthur, due to work commitments but when he did, Arthur seemed to be affectionate to all his children. James had seen the family go out for walks with Beatrice carrying one of the twins and Arthur carrying the other. Finally, during the time the family lived with him, James had heard no arguments.

A suggestion that Devereux might have had financial concerns was outlined by the next witness, Frederick George Turner. Frederick was the proprietor of a chemist shop situated at Princess Road, Kilburn. He testified that he had placed a newspaper advertisement for an assistant in May 1904. A reply had been received from Devereux and, as a result, the prisoner had been employed from 28 May, at another shop owned by Mr Turner at Fernhead Road. Devereux had been a good worker but unfortunately, business was not as good as expected and, on 2 January 1905, Mr Turner had to give Devereux one month's notice. His last day of employment was 27 January 1905. This, of course, was the day before Beatrice had last been seen alive, by her mother, Ellen Gregory.

The court had already heard that the Devereux family had lodged at 23 Malvern Road until 31 December 1904. On that same day they had moved into 60 Milton Avenue. The owner of that property was William Garfath, and he explained that the house was divided into two flats. Shortly before Christmas 1904, Devereux had called on Mr Garfath at his home at 24 Shelley Road, Harlesden and explained that he was interested in renting one of the flats. On Christmas Eve, Devereux called again and said he wished to take the top floor flat. He explained that he would only require the flat for some six weeks or so as he would be moving out in February. He then made a rather strange request from his new landlord. Devereux explained that he had a little boy and did not wish him to mix with other children. As a result, he would be grateful if Mr Garfath kept the ground floor flat free.

This evidence was held to be highly significant. In the first place, Devereux had only mentioned having one child. In addition, he had already said that he intended moving out in six weeks or so and he had asked that the other flat be left empty. Was that really because he did not want prying neighbours disturbing the plans he had already made to dispose of his wife and two youngest sons?

In part, this significance was reduced when William Garfath went on to say that he had spent a good deal of time in the area of Milton Avenue, on business, and had seen Devereux out with his twins. At around 11.00am on 7 February, Mr Garfath had again been in Milton Avenue and had seen the furniture van from Bannister's at the house. Devereux had explained that he was moving some boxes into a furnished apartment. That same evening, Mr Garfath was back at Milton Avenue and saw a second van at number 60, being loaded with tables and chairs. Concerned that his tenant might be moving without paying the rent he owed, William Garfath spoke to Devereux about all this movement. Devereux said he thought it better to move into his new furnished apartments as soon as possible, explained that he was selling his own furniture and would pay the 7s 6d rent he owed as soon as the items were sold.

More details of the Devereux's stay at 60 Milton Avenue were given by Sarah Wells, who lived next door at number 58. She recalled the family moving in to number 60 and reported that they seemed to be quiet and ordinary. At the beginning of February she heard noises coming from next door which sounded as if someone were taking furniture to pieces. This was explained a day or so later when the Bannister's van appeared and the various items of furniture were loaded on to it. Finally, Mrs Wells was able to say that although she saw Devereux and his eldest son leaving with the van, there was no sign of Beatrice or the twins.

In the course of their daily lives at 60 Milton Avenue, the Devereux family received various deliveries. Horace Furlong was a baker who delivered bread to Devereux and he told the court that he began calling at number 60 on 6 January. From that date onwards he called every day, except Sunday, at some time between noon and 1.00pm. Usually, it was Mrs Devereux who came to the door, and Furlong last saw her on Saturday 28 January.

The next time Furlong called was on Monday 30 January. This time there was no answer to his knocking so he left the bread on the front doorstep. The next day, Tuesday, there was again no answer to his calling but this time he did not leave any bread, thinking that the family might have moved out. The next day, 1 February, it was Stanley who answered the door, and took the bread in. Once again there was no answer on either 2 February or the 3rd but on Saturday 4 February, it was Devereux himself who answered the door. By this time the total bill was close on three shillings and Furlong asked Devereux for the money. He replied that he would call in at the shop at 1 Park Parade and pay the balance in full but, in the event, he never did call. Furlong did call at the house a couple of times the following week, but never found anyone home.

Further evidence relating to deliveries was given by Harry Brazier, a dairyman who delivered milk to Milton Avenue. He had last seen Mrs Devereux on 23 January but of more significance was his evidence relating to what Arthur Devereux had told him at a later date.

At around 5.00pm on Monday 30 January, Brazier had called to collect the seven shillings he was owed. Devereux answered the door and said that his wife was responsible for paying but she had just gone out and would call into the shop the next day to settle the bill. On the afternoon of the next day, 31 January, Devereux told Brazier not to deliver any more milk and told him that his wife had gone away.

From the evidence given so far, the implication was that Beatrice Devereux, and therefore presumably the twins, had all died at some time after 11.00pm on Saturday 28 January, when she had parted from her mother, but some time before Furlong the baker had called, on the morning of Monday 30 January.

Assuming that Devereux now had three bodies on his hands, which he needed to dispose of, how could he do so whilst Stanley, his eldest son, was still in the house? A possible answer was given by Amy Jackson and her sister, Georgina. They ran a small school for boys from 3 Manor Villas, Acton Lane and they recalled

Deveraux calling on a Saturday night to place Stanley at the school. From the next Monday onwards, Stanley was dropped off at 9.00am, taken out by his father at noon, returned at 1.00pm and then taken home when school had finished for the day. Unfortunately, neither lady could state with accuracy when this arrangement began, only saying that it was on a Saturday either at the end of January or the beginning of February. What they could say was that it was around 7.45pm on that Saturday when Devereux had called.

Details of Devereux selling his furniture were given by the next two witnesses: Thomas Perry and Susan Flint. Perry was a partner in the firm of Shallis and Co of 30 Manor Park Road and he testified that Devereux had called on him at 4.00pm on Saturday 4 February, with a perambulator which he wished to sell. They also discussed furniture and as a result, Perry called at Milton Avenue the following Monday. He purchased various items and collected them the next day.

Perry did not deal in wardrobes so had given Susan Flint's name to Devereux as he knew her to deal in such items. Devereux had called on her a day or so later and sold her some women's clothing, some baby items and a wardrobe.

Edward Lewis Gardiner was a builder who lived at 18 Craven Road, Harlesden and some time around the beginning of February he received a visit from Devereux who asked him for a sheet of zinc. A deal was made and Devereux went away with the zinc that same day, having paid 1s 6d for it.

Hedley Egbert Dwelly was a chemist trading from premises at 41 Acton Lane. He told the court that on Saturday 4 February, he had sold a four ounce bottle of carbolic acid to Devereux.

The next witness was John Tabboth who lived at 92 Harrow Road, with his wife Ada. Tabboth had advertised a room to let and on 6 February, Devereux had called to ask about it. There was only one bed in the room and Devereux said that he would need another as he had a little boy, who was aged five. He explained that he had two more children, twin boys, but his wife was away in the country and had taken them with her. He would only need the room for about a fortnight.

One of the letters Devereux sent to Bannister's to ask after the tin trunk.
The National Archives

Devereux and his son remained a lodger until 20 February when he left to take up a new position in Coventry. Devereux had asked Tabboth if Stanley could stay on until he found suitable lodgings. Tabboth agreed and, as a result, various letters passed between the two men until finally, on 22 March, arrangements were made to send Stanley to Coventry on the 1.30pm train from Euston.

Thomas Bannister was the next witness to give evidence. He stated that he was a furniture mover and contractor trading from premises at 591 Harrow Road, with a warehouse at Buller Road. On 7 February, he had sent two men, Allingham and Willoughby, to 60 Milton Avenue to move some furniture for the occupant. In due course, they returned with a tin trunk and five shillings to pay for storage at Buller Road and the hire of the van. The trunk was duly put in a loft, where it remained undisturbed until 13 April. During that time, Ellen Gregory had called five or six times but Bannister had not given her any details about where Devereux had moved on to, though one of his employees might have done so eventually.

One of the letters Mr Bannister received. Note the early mention of the tin trunk. The National Archives

Bannister had mentioned two of his employees who had moved items from 60 Milton Avenue to 92 Harrow Road, and collected the tin trunk for storage. Since these events, one of those men, Henry Allingham, had died from pneumonia. Inspector Edwin Pollard had, however, interviewed Allingham and had taken a statement from him. That statement was now read out in court, by Pollard himself.

The statement began: 'On the 7th February, I went with Willoughby and a van to 60 Milton Avenue. I assisted in loading up the van with the boxes and a tin trunk. I accompanied the van to 92 Harrow Road, and afterwards we went to the Warwick public house. Prisoner was with us.'

'The van was then paid for and five shillings was presented to Willoughby. Prisoner said he wanted the tin trunk warehoused at Mr Bannister's. My mate wanted to know the name. Prisoner said "No name, I do not want you to let my mother-in-law know where the boxes were brought to." We then drove to the *Flora* public house and had some drink and the prisoner left us.'

'We took the box to Mr Bannister's. A mark of a cross was put on the box in the yard. Two days afterwards, 9 February, I again saw the prisoner. He spoke to me. He said "I want to know if I can see the box at any time, because I am going to sell it as soon as I can get a chemist to buy it." I told him it was in the top warehouse. He gave me a shilling. The little boy was with him.'

To this point in the proceedings, little real damage had been done to Devereux's defence. He, it must be remembered, was claiming that Beatrice had killed the twins and herself and he had mistakenly disposed of the bodies. To strengthen his case, Mr Elliott for the defence now recalled Ellen Gregory, the dead woman's mother.

In effect, her evidence was somewhat contradictory. She began by saying that when Devereux and her daughter had first met, at Hastings in 1896, it seemed to be a love match. Beatrice was devoted to him and he was very much attached to her. Ellen then went on to discuss Sidney Gregory, her son and Beatrice's brother. Ellen confirmed that Sidney had, at one stage, suffered from meningitis. He recovered, married a lady named Florence Manning and they then moved to Plymouth. On 28 July 1903, Sidney had written to Ellen but that was the last time she had ever heard from him. Soon afterwards his clothing had been found on Plymouth Hoe and it was presumed that he had drowned himself at sea. This greatly affected Beatrice who had been very close to her brother. She began to object that her husband seemed to show more affection for Stanley than he did for the twins. The relationship between Ellen and Devereux cooled appreciably and he objected to her calling at the house so that eventually she would only call when she knew he was at work.

After this interlude, the prosecution called their next witness, George Willoughby, the surviving carman from Bannister's. He confirmed that he and Allingham had arrived at 60 Milton Avenue at around 11.00am. The only people there were Devereux and his son, Stanley. The two carmen moved various boxes and a tin trunk which had been kept in the back room upstairs. This was very heavy and Devereux told him that it contained chemicals and books.

The time came to hear the medical evidence. Dr Augustus Joseph Pepper had, with Dr George Robertson, made post-mortem examinations on all three bodies. He began by detailing how the bodies had been placed into the tin trunk.

Beatrice Devereux was lying on her left side with her head bent down onto her chest and her thighs and legs flexed. Her body bore slight marks of bruising received before death. A subsequent examination showed that she had died from asphyxia but there was no evidence as to how she had been asphyxiated.

Turning to the twins, Dr Pepper stated that Lawrence was lying face downwards between the thighs and legs of his mother. There were no marks of violence on his body and the only sign of disease was that of rickets. He had also died from asphyxia. The other boy, Evelyn, was lying huddled up the same way as his brother. Again there were no external marks of violence and death was due to asphyxia.

One other important point was then raised. It had taken some considerable manipulation to place the bodies so that they would fit into the trunk. That meant that the bodies had been flexible so rigor mortis would not have set in. This in turn meant that they had been put into the trunk within twelve hours or so of death.

The next few witnesses all referred to points of evidence already made. Thus, Thomas Sims confirmed details of Devereux visiting Bannister's to check on the tin trunk left in storage whilst Henry Crawford and Charles Rogers spoke of various minor items of women's clothing and children's items they had purchased from the prisoner. Finally, James Miller, a book-dealer of 479 Harrow Road, confirmed that he had purchased some books from him.

Of more import was the testimony of Frederick Bird, a chemist at 156 Spon Street, Coventry. At the beginning of February he had placed an advertisement in the Chemist and Druggist asking for an assistant. On 17 February he had received a letter from Devereux, applying for that position. The letter read:

Dear Sir, I note your advertisement in the Chemist and Druggist, and beg to offer myself for the berth.
I am thirty years of age, 5 feet 11 inches tall, and possess the minor

*qualifications. I am now disengaged and require £50 as salary.
I have been during the past five years with Mr Taylor of 479
Harrow Road and was formerly with the late Mr Marshall of
Sloane Square and Streatham Hill. Any further particulars I shall
be pleased to give you upon application. I have just left my last
berth to make room for my employer's son.*

Mr Bird replied and received a second letter on 19 February. As
a result, a reference was taken and a reply received by telegram
which read:

'Devereux good man suit your requirements.'

Devereux was then taken on, at the salary he had requested, and
remained in Mr Bird's employ until his arrest on 13 April.

Details of that arrest were given by Mr Charles Christopher
Charsley, the Chief Constable of Coventry. He had gone to Mr
Bird's shop on 13 April and told Devereux that he was to be
arrested on suspicion of murder. Mr Bird was present and said:
'Devereux, I am sorry to hear of this,' to which the prisoner had
replied: 'It is all right Mr Bird, I can clear myself.'

Inspector Pollard was now called to give evidence on his own
behalf. He stated that, acting on information received from Ellen
Gregory, he had gone to Bannister's warehouse on 13 April.
Retrieving the tin trunk, his men had first shaken it in order to
determine if it might contain chemicals as had been stated. There
was no vibration, suggesting that the contents were tightly packed
together. The trunk was opened, and the various layers removed
until a child's head was finally revealed. The bodies were not
disturbed at that time, but photographs were taken.

That same evening, Pollard and Sergeant George Cole travelled
to Coventry and early the next morning, 14 April, they had seen
Devereux, who was in custody at Coventry police station.
Devereux was told about the finding of the bodies and then taken
back to London. On the train, Devereux said he wished to make
a statement, but Pollard's pen ran out of ink and was advised to
wait until he got back to London.

Later that same day, 14 April, Devereux made his statement at Harlesden police station. It read:

I, Arthur Devereux, hereby declare that one evening towards the end of January or beginning of February last, having been out for a few hours with my child Stanley, I returned to find my wife and twins lying dead in their beds, evidently, to my mind, having died from poison taken or administered.

Rather than face an inquest I decided, with a recent trial fresh in my mind, to conceal the bodies in a trunk which I had had in my possession for about two years. This I proceeded to do at once.

I missed some poisons, chloroform and morphia, which I always kept in my writing desk after leaving my last situation, in the event of my wishing to end my own life, rather than face starvation. The room smelled strongly of chloroform so I concluded that my wife had administered it to herself and the children, probably also the morphia. I had had a violent quarrel with her previously to going out; also many times quite recently and during the past twelve months.

I make this statement quite voluntarily, without any threats having been made or promises held out to me. I wished to make it when first detained at Coventry, but was advised not to do so.

Various specimens had been taken from the three bodies, and these had been sent on to Sir Thomas Stevenson, the official analyst to the Home Office. He had also examined a number of items from the trunk, including handkerchiefs. Blood, mucus and epithelia cells had been found on those handkerchiefs, suggesting that they might have been used for wiping the mouths of the victims either before or after death.

Turning to the various internal organs, Sir Thomas had found morphine in the stomach, abdomen, liver and kidneys but he was unable to say how it had been administered. He was able to estimate, from the quantities he had found, that the original dose would have been around four grains. The effect of this would be an initial state of excitement, followed by a tendency to sleep. Within around three to six hours, death would occur and the post-mortem would indicate death by asphyxia. Finally, there was no evidence of chloroform being administered to any of the three bodies.

At that, the prosecution case closed. The suggestion was that Devereux, whilst fond of his eldest son, had not been affectionate towards his sick twins. Having lost his job in London, he knew that they would be a financial burden upon him and that he would have a far better chance of obtaining a new position if he represented himself as a single man with just one child. Thus, possibly after an argument over Beatrice being out with her mother again, he had murdered her and the twins, disposed of their bodies and escaped to Coventry. The time had come for the defence to put forward an alternative explanation of what had taken place at 60 Milton Avenue.

The first witness for the defence was Arthur Devereux himself. He stated that on 31 January, he had been out with Stanley and they returned home at around 9.00pm. Before he had left, he and Beatrice had argued and she had told him that when he returned, he would find her and the twins gone.

Upon entering the house there was a strong smell of chloroform and his first instinct was to open a window. As he lifted the blinds he saw his wife lying on their bed with the twins apparently asleep inside their cots. Upon checking, he found all three of them dead and surmised that Beatrice had first killed the twins and then herself.

After putting Stanley to bed, Devereux had then got the tin trunk and packed the bodies into it after placing it in the back bedroom. They were still warm as he placed them inside. The next morning he told Stanley that his mother had been taken into hospital and the twins were staying at a nursery whilst she was there. Stanley was then taken to school and whilst he was there, Devereux tried to solder zinc over the top of the bodies to make it airtight. He failed in that effort so placed tightly fitting wooden planks over them instead. Finally, he had lied in his letters to Mr Bird about being a widower with one son because it was harder for a married man to obtain a new position.

It would be for the jury to decide if Devereux were a cold-blooded killer or if his wife was unstable enough to have behaved as he had suggested. Other witnesses were now called to shed more light on the possible behaviour of Beatrice Devereux, and also on the mental strengths or otherwise of the prisoner himself.

Julia Maria Devereux was the prisoner's aunt and she was called to give evidence that showed that Arthur Devereux might well have behaved irrationally after discovering three bodies in his home. Mr Justice Ridley interrupted to ask Mr Elliott for clearance and having been told why this witness had been called, the judge rather showed his own thoughts by stating, in front of the jury, that he could not see that this evidence could be of the slightest value.

Julia Devereux was allowed to give her testimony, however, and she stated that in 1862, her father, had tried to kill himself by hanging. In 1891, her brother, the prisoner's father, who was also named Arthur, had also tried to take his own life. Another member of the family had thrown herself out of a window in Regent's Park in 1883.

Louis Devereux was the prisoner's brother. At one stage they had lodged together at Highbury and during that time, Arthur had caused him a good deal of concern. He had once stayed out for three nights, and slept in Finsbury Park. Eventually, a doctor was called in and Arthur was sent away to rest. The doctor referred to was a Dr Sworn but when Mr Elliott for the defence stated that he did not intend to call Dr Sworn, the judge held that this evidence was also of no value.

Dr Humphrey Wheeler told the court that he had attended Caleb Devereux, the prisoner's uncle, in 1895 and certified him as insane. He had also attended Caleb's daughter, who was Devereux's cousin, and she too had been treated for insanity.

The Devereux family had originally come from Penn in Buckinghamshire, and the vicar there was Benjamin John Short Kirkby. He testified that he had known the family for many years. He had known the prisoner as a boy and considered him wanting in many ways. Devereux had been described, the local euphemism as a 'little bit off the top'. He had behaved in extreme ways. Once he had represented himself as an American millionaire. On another occasion he had posed as a magician and said he would give a show. The hall was very crowded but Devereux just stood in front of them and did nothing. His only trick was to make the audience vanish very quickly!

Dr Forbes Winslow was an expert on lunacy and, at the request of the defence, had made a personal examination of the prisoner. At this, Mr Matthews objected for the prosecution stating that it was for the jury to decide if the prisoner were insane. Startlingly, after some discussion, Mr Justice Ridley ruled that Dr Winslow's evidence was inadmissible and ought not to be accepted but, as a matter of indulgence, he would accept it. This was an astonishing statement for a judge to make in a murder trial.

Finally giving his testimony, Dr Winslow said he had examined Devereux, on two occasions, at Brixton prison in the presence of three other medical men: Dr Scott, Dr McCarthy and Dr Armstrong. Various tests had been applied and questions put to the prisoner and in conclusion, Dr Winslow believed Devereux to be of very weak intellect, suffering from partial mental disease but would know the difference between right and wrong.

Two of the other doctors mentioned also gave evidence. Dr John Armstrong agreed with Dr Winslow's evidence, as did Dr Eugene Talbot McCarthy who added that he did not believe that Devereux had the same reasoning powers as an average man.

Mary Francis Gregory was married to Beatrice Devereux's brother, Sidney. In May 1903 she had noticed that Sidney seemed to be very white in colour and when she asked him what the matter was, he said that he was feeling the heat very much. From that day on his behaviour seemed to change and he suffered from headaches a lot.

On Saturday 25 July 1903, Sidney said that his head was very bad indeed. Mary had bathed it for him. Soon afterwards he went out for an hour or so but later still he left the house again and did not return. His clothes were found on Plymouth Hoe that evening. No body was ever found and whilst Mary believed that Sidney was dead, her mother-in-law, Ellen Gregory, believed that he was still alive and she would see him again one day. This testimony was confirmed by Mary's brother, Edgar Manning, who had gone to stay with the Devereuxs in Plymouth. He described Mary and Sidney as being very happy together and saw no reason for Sidney to have taken his own life.

The final witness was Annie Elizabeth Harries who lived at 10 Elgin Avenue, Notting Hill. She had known Beatrice Devereux for some time. In 1899, Beatrice had called on Annie Harries. At the time, Stanley was only a small baby and the two women chatted about children in general.

Beatrice told Annie that if it hadn't been for her mother, she would not have got through having this baby. She was very depressed and this hadn't been helped by the fact that her father had just gone through bankruptcy, and during the hearing a terrible disclosure had been made about him living with a servant and having three children with her. The whole affair had nearly killed her mother.

It was plain that having financial concerns greatly worried Beatrice and she confessed openly to Annie that if she ever faced the same sort of problem she would rather commit suicide and take Stanley with her, rather than leave him to the mercies of the world. Unfortunately, the prosecution were able to greatly diminish Annie's testimony by showing that she had been confined to various mental institutions between 1899 and 1905.

We have already seen how the trial judge, Mr Justice Ridley, had behaved improperly towards the testimony of some of the defence witnesses. In his summing up, this same gentleman made a most astounding observation. He stated, quite openly, that he saw no reason for Beatrice to have killed her children and then taken her own life. This was astonishing because if Arthur Devereux were guilty then his motive must have been financial concerns after he lost his job. Surely Beatrice would have had exactly the same concerns and therefore, exactly the same motives.

In the event, the jury took just ten minutes to decide that Devereux was guilty as charged, whereupon he was sentenced to death. There was no appeal and no reprieve and on Tuesday 15 August, Arthur Devereux as hanged at Pentonville prison by

H.O. REGISTRY
345
15 AUG 1905
RECEIVED

13149
14

Surrey House
Victoria Embankment
W.C.
15th August 1905.

Sir

I beg to inform you that Arthur Devereux was this morning executed in H. M. Prison of Pentonville in accordance with the sentence of Death passed upon him by The Honble Mr. Justice Ridley

I beg also to report that the Execution was carried out in a satisfactory manner

I enclose:—

(1) The Declaration of the Sheriff & others

(2) The Certificate of the Surgeon

(3) The Inquisition of the Coroner and others

I have the honour to be
Sir
Your obedient Servant

Confirmation of Devereux's execution. The National Archives

Henry Pierrepoint and John Ellis. Devereux's last words, just before he left the condemned cell were:

I have nothing to add to what I have already said.

In an English court, it is not for the defence to prove innocence, it is for the prosecution to prove guilt beyond a reasonable doubt. Arthur Devereux may well have murdered his wife and twin sons but there is at least an argument that his wife might well have been responsible. Surely Devereux's own mental instability would have caused him to behave in exactly the way he described after finding three bodies in his flat after returning from a walk. Added to this, the behaviour of the trial judge is tantamount to misdirection, and that alone should have been enough to secure a commutation of the death sentence to one of life imprisonment.

Chapter 3

Steinie Morrison

1911

At approximately 8.10am on the morning of Sunday 1 January 1911, Constable Joseph Mumford was patrolling his usual beat on Clapham Common. As he strolled along the pathway, which led from the bandstand towards Lavender Gardens, he saw the body of a man lying amongst some bushes, but close to the path itself. The man was well-dressed. He wore an expensive looking coat, trimmed with astrakhan, and had on leather boots. He was lying on his back and had apparently been severely beaten. A trail of blood led from some railings and a hat, which presumably belonged to the victim, lay some twelve feet to the south. The only way in which Mumford disturbed the scene at all, was by lifting the man's left hand in order to check for a pulse. The constable found none and, replacing the hand, he went to summon assistance.

Less than an hour later, at 9.00am, Dr Joseph Needham, the police surgeon, arrived at the scene. He noted down an initial description of the body showing that a black handkerschief was drawn over the top of the head, covering the ears on both sides. A number of severe wounds were noted on and around the head. Further, the pulled-up position of the coat collar led Dr Needham to conclude that the man had been dragged by that collar, face downwards, to the position where he now lay. From the temperature of the body, Dr Needham believed that the time of death was some six hours before, putting it at around 3.00am on New Year's Day.

The body was moved to the mortuary where some police photographs were taken. The various injuries on the body were noted, including two strange S-shaped cuts, one to each cheek.

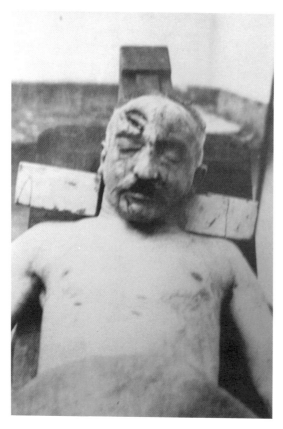

The body of Leon Beron, photographed at the mortuary. The National Archives

The man had certainly been beaten but there were also three deep stab wounds to the chest. As for the motive for this crime, that appeared to be quite clear, for although this was obviously a man of some means, only one single halfpenny was found on his body.

The officer in charge of the investigation was Detective Inspector Alfred Ward. He found no form of identification amongst the man's belongings, but he did find a notebook with a large list of names, most of them foreign sounding. Further, the majority of the names were of women and lists of regular payments made by them suggested that this book was actually a rent book. It might well be that the victim had been a local landlord.

Amongst the other items found upon the body was an envelope addressed to Mr Israel Iglazer at 16 Coke Street, Whitechapel. Another officer on the case, Detective Inspector Frederick Porter Wensley was sent to interview Mr Iglazer, even though Wensley was heavily involved with the investigation into the Houndsditch murders. This was an event which had taken place on 16 December 1910, when anarchists had shot dead three policemen and was obviously taking up a great deal of police time.

Wensley duly traced Mr Iglazer who, given a description of the dead man, was able to give another address, 133 Jubilee Street, where he believed the victim had resided with his brother. Officers were then sent to that address, but when there was no answer to their knocking, the door was forced.

The inside of the single room was absolutely filthy but a careful search was made and various papers were discovered, including a photograph of the dead man. The police were now certain that they did have the correct address and now only had to wait for the brother of the dead man to come home.

It was not until the early hours of 2 January that Solomon Beron returned to his home at 133 Jubilee Street, to find two police officers waiting to interview him. Shown the photograph, he confirmed that this was his brother. Solomon was then taken to the mortuary to make a positive identification of the body and now, finally, the victim had a name; forty-eight-year-old Leon Beron.

Leon Beron had been born in Russia but his family had moved to France when he was still a baby. He then lived there for some thirty years until the family moved on again, this time to London. It was then 1894. Leon purchased a number of small houses; nine in all, and earned his living from the rents. His brother estimated that Leon had an income of some £25 a year but he had not had a bank account, preferring to keep all his money on his person. Solomon Beron estimated that at the time of his death, Leon should have had around £12 in cash on him. Further, it appeared that other items were also unaccounted for. Leon had owned a gold watch and chain and attached to this chain was a gold £5 piece. Finally, Solomon was able to say that he had last seen Leon alive at around 10.45pm on 31 December, in Fieldgate Street. He had been alone at the time.

Further police investigation revealed that Leon Beron was perhaps not all that he initially appeared to be. It was true that he owned nine properties but these were little more than slums, largely rented out to prostitutes, and would only have brought him a few shillings each week. Yet Beron was never short of money, and always wore expensive clothes. Though he had no criminal record, there were suspicions that Beron might have supplemented his income by dealing in stolen property. That, however, was now of no concern. The only thing the police were interested in was finding his killer or killers.

The newspapers were filled with stories of the Houndsditch murders and this new crime was, at least in the eyes of the press, soon linked with that outrage. After all, there were those curious S-shaped cuts on Beron's cheeks. Why would a robber have bothered to inflict such a wound? Surely it was a sign, a warning perhaps. There were suggestions that this cut had been left as a brand, by anarchists, to show that they believed Beron was a police informer. The police were forced to issue denials. They had never had any previous dealings with Beron, he had not been an informer and this was simply a case of robbery and murder.

It was important now to trace Leon Beron's movements from the time he left his home on 31 December. By now, Inspector Ward had discovered that one of Beron's favourite haunts was Snelwar's Warsaw Restaurant at 32 Osborn Street, Whitechapel.

The restaurant was run by Alec Snelwar who confirmed that Beron had been a regular customer for more than six years. Of more significance perhaps, was the fact that over the past three weeks or so, Beron had spent a great deal of time in company with another man. This man had first started coming into the restaurant about two months before but had recently become acquainted with Beron. Now they were together every single day, usually some time between 9.00pm and 10.00pm.

On 31 December 1910, Beron had first come into Snelwar's at about 2.00pm but left soon afterwards. He was back at 9.00pm when he was with his new found acquaintance. They were in conversation until 11.45pm when they left together. Snelwar had never seen Beron again but his friend had been back the next day, 1 January, between 11.00am and noon. He did not purchase anything but simply walked into the centre of the restaurant, looked around and then left again. He had not been back since.

Alec Snelwar had one more interesting piece of information for the police. On the night of 31 December, the man with Beron had

had a long, thin, brown paper parcel with him, which he said was a flute. At one stage, Snelwar's ten-year-old daughter Becky had playfully picked up the parcel and it was clear that it was much too heavy to be a flute. Finally, from talking to other customers, Inspector Ward was able to put a name to Leon Beron's companion. The man he had been talking to was known by various names including Moses Tagger and Morris Stein but he preferred to go by the name of Steinie Morrison.

A police check on Steinie Morrison revealed some interesting facts. Morrison had been born in the Ukraine in 1879 and had first come to England in 1898. Almost from the outset he was in trouble with the police. In December 1898, he had been given a one month prison sentence for theft. Since then he had been in trouble many more times and he had served two five-year sentences; one in 1901 and another in 1906. He had only been released from that last sentence on 17 September 1910.

In September that release from prison had been on licence and that carried certain conditions, one of which was that Morrison had to keep the police informed where he was living. According to the records he had taken a job at Pither's Bakery at 213 Lavender Hill and had been lodging at 26 Grove Street. However, when that information was checked, officers found that Morrison had quit his job after just six weeks and was no longer living in Grove Street. Those actions meant that Morrison was in breach of his licence and could be arrested on that charge once he was traced.

In fact, it did not take long to trace Morrison. His new address was 91 Newark Street where he rented a room from Annie and Maurice Zimmerman. Unfortunately, when Inspector Ward called at that address he found that Annie Zimmerman hadn't seen Morrison since the morning of 1 January. Further enquiries revealed that when he had left his lodgings, Morrison had exhibited some rather unusual behaviour.

From Newark Street Morrison had gone to St Mary's Station where he had deposited a parcel in the left luggage office, using yet another name: Banman. From St Mary's he had gone to Walworth Road where he had called on Max Frank, a jeweller, and changed £10 worth of gold sovereigns for treasury notes. It was known that Leon Beron liked to keep his money in the form of sovereigns so his killer would have such coins in his possession. A watch was placed on Newark Street and officers waited for Morrison to return to his lodgings.

On the morning of 8 January, the two officers detailed to watch Morrison's lodgings were Detective Constable Harry Jeffries and Detective Constable James Bellinger. It was 9.20am when they finally saw Morrison walk down the street and go into number 91. He was carrying a brown paper parcel and a walking stick. Within minutes, Morrison was back on the street and the two constables followed him to Cohen's Restaurant at 7 Fieldgate Street. A message was sent to headquarters and soon afterwards Inspector Wensley and Detective Sergeant William Brogden joined their colleagues. All four police officers then entered the restaurant, identified themselves to Morrison who was seated at a table near the door, and told him he was wanted for questioning. The prisoner was then escorted to Leman Street police station.

A brief interview led Morrison to state that for the past few days he had been living with Florrie Delton, a prostitute, at 116 York Road. Sergeant Brodgen and Inspector Ward visited that address and took away various items including some clothing. Later still, the clothing Morrison was wearing was taken for examination. That examination found blood on the left cuff of Morrison's shirt, and also on his collar and tie. The following day, 9 January, Morrison was told that he would be charged with the murder of Leon Beron. It was a charge he strenuously denied.

Steinie Morrison appeared at the Old Bailey on 6 March 1911, before Mister Justice Darling. The trial would last until 15 March, during which time the case for the Crown was led by Mr Richard D Muir, who was assisted by Mr William Leycester and Mr Ingleby Oddie. Morrison was defended by Mr Edward Abinger who was originally assisted by Mr Alasdair MacGregor. Four days into the trial, Mr MacGregor fell ill and he was replaced by Mr Roland Oliver.

During the early days, the police investigation had centred around the questions of how Beron and his killer had got to

Clapham Common and how the killer had escaped afterwards. It was reasonable to assume that the men had taken cabs, so word was spread that a reward of £1 would be paid to any cab-driver with information. This brought forward three men.

The first of these was Alfred Stephens who told the investigation that he had picked up two men at the *Royal Hotel*, Blackfriars and taken them to Cedar Road, Clapham Common, arriving there at around 1.30am on 1 January. After dropping the two men off, Stephens parked his cab at the rank at Clapham Cross. He remained there until 2.30am when he a man approached him and asked to be taken to Kennington.

This passenger had been dropped off at the *Hanover* public house and was last seen walking towards another public house, the *Horns*. Stephens described this man as five feet ten inches tall, clean-shaven and with a darkish complexion. On 9 January he had seen a picture of Morrison in the newspaper and was sure this was the man. Further, he attended the police court on 17 January and picked Morrison from a line-up of men.

The second cab driver was Edward Hayman. He testified that he had picked up two men on the corner of Sidney Street and Mile End Road at 2.00am on 1 January.

He was certain that one of these men was Morrison and described the other as five feet five inches tall, and wearing a dark overcoat and a bowler hat. The two men were taken to Lavender Gardens, on the Clapham Junction side, and it was Morrison who paid the fare. On 17 January, Hayman had attended an identification parade and picked out Morrison.

The final driver was Alfred Castling. He had been parked at the rank at Kennington Church at 3.30am on 1 January when two men approached him. The two were taken to Seven Sisters Road. Castling had since attended an identification parade at Leman Street police station on 9 January and had picked out Morrison as one of the passengers.

What was the value of the testimony of these three witnesses which seemed to show Morrison and Beron taking cabs all over London during the early hours of 1 January? One factor that might suggest an answer is that none of these men came forward until after the police had posted notices of a reward for information. In addition, all three admitted that they had seen pictures of Morrison before they attended their respective identity parades. Finally, during those parades, none of the other men were as tall as Morrison, making him stand out like a beacon. Could it be that the police were in some way assisting these witnesses?

The next set of witnesses all came from the Snelwar Restaurant. Alec Snelwar told the court of Morrison's many meetings with Beron during the weeks prior to the latter's death. He was also able to say that it was common knowledge that Beron always carried a good deal of money and that he was proud of the gold watch he habitually wore. Indeed, Beron often handed his watch to people so that they could feel the weight of it. On one occasion, he had seen Morrison holding the watch in his hand.

Joe Mintz was a waiter at the restaurant, having started there on 1 December 1910. He had known Beron prior to this, probably for around two years and he too confirmed that Morrison had become a regular customer over the last few weeks of December. Morrison got on very well with Snelwar's daughter, Becky. He was also able to tell the court of the heavy parcel which apparently had contained a flute.

One of the other regular customers at Snelwar's was Harry Hermelin, who actually had lodgings above the restaurant. He told the court that on 31 December, Morrison was already in the restaurant when Beron came in and sat next to him.

Sam Rosen was another customer at the restaurant and on 31 December he saw Morrison and Beron together. They were still in conversation there when Rosen left at 11.30pm. Rosen had, however, seen the two men together later still. At some time between 12.30am and 1.30am, he saw them at the corner of Brick Lane, walking towards Sidney Street. This dovetailed neatly with the earlier testimony of the cabman Edward Hayman, who had reported picking the two men up in Sidney Street at 2.00am, but there was a major problem with this evidence.

At the police court hearing, Rosen had told a somewhat different story, saying that he had no idea what time he had seen the two men heading towards Sidney Street. He now confirmed that Solomon Beron had told him he must stick to the time of 1.30am or he might risk going to prison. Rosen said he had also been threatened by Solomon and others.

Jack Taw was a sixteen-year-old part-time waiter at the restaurant and although he had not been on duty on the night of 31 December, he had called in at around 11.15pm and seen Morrison and Beron together. Later still, at 1.45am on 1 January, Taw had been sitting at a coffee stall on the corner of Church Lane when he saw Morrison and Beron walking together in Whitechapel Road. Yet, under cross-examination, Taw had to confirm that he had not been to the police with his story until he had first tried to sell it to the newspapers.

Another witness who claimed to have seen Beron and Morrison together was Jacob Weissberg. He said he had first seen them at 7.30pm on 31 December when they were at the corner of Tucker Street and Commercial Street. Weissberg said he had then seen them again, at 12.45am on 1 January, in Whitechapel Road. He was able to say that this last time was exact as he noticed the time by the church clock.

Yet another sighting had been made by Nellie Deitch who lived in Commercial Road, Whitechapel, at number 401. She told the court that she had known Beron for many years. In fact, Leon had once lodged with her father, in Brick Lane in the 1890s.

On the night of 31 December, Nellie was at a party at 73 Commercial Street. At around 1.15am on 1 January, she left to go home and saw Beron between Bedford Street and Philpot Street. He was with another man, whom she did not know, but she did get a good look at him. She too had had no hesitation in picking out Morrison as this companion at a subsequent identity parade. This evidence must, however, be taken with a goodly pinch of salt since in her original statement to the police, Nellie had put this sighting at 3.00am. She could offer no explanation as to why she had now changed the time to 1.15am.

Before passing to the evidence of the various police officers in this case, we should perhaps condense the many sightings made of Beron and Morrison together. If we assume, for the moment, that all the witnesses were being truthful, then we have the following summary of the movements of the events of that fateful night:

31 December
7.30pm   – Corner of Tucker Street and Commercial Street
              (Jacob Weissberg)
11.30pm – In Snelwar's Restaurant (Various)
11.45pm – They leave the restaurant together (Various)

1 January
12.45am – Whitechapel Road (Jacob Weissberg)
1.15am   – Commercial Street (Nellie Deitch)
1.30am   – Brick Lane towards Sidney Street (Sam Rosen)
1.45am   – Whitechapel Road (Jack Taw)
2.00am   – Cab from Sidney Street/Mile End Road to
              Lavender Gardens (Edward Hayman)
2.30am   – Morrison goes from Clapham Cross to
              Kennington in cab (Alfred Stephens)
3.30am   – Kennington church to Seven Sisters Road in cab
              (Alfred Castling)

Are we really expected to believe that Morrison and Beron spent the best part of two and a half hours apparently walking round the streets of Whitechapel before taking three rapid journeys in cabs?

The police had made a strong point of the fact that when he had been arrested, no mention of a murder had been made by any officer but Morrison had immediately begun to talk about a murder charge against him. How could he have known that he was suspected of a murder before the police mentioned it, unless of course, he knew in advance and was therefore guilty.

Constable Jeffries, one of the officers who had been watching Morison's lodgings said that no mention of the word murder was made in his hearing right up to the time Morrison was interviewed at Leman Street. However, this officer had said at an earlier hearing at the police court that he did not know himself that Morrison was wanted for murder. He now had to admit that he had known all along and claimed that his earlier testimony was a slip. He further admitted that it was customary to tell an arrested man why he was wanted but claimed that this had not been done in Morrison's case.

Inspector Ward told the court that when he had viewed the body of Leon Beron in situ on Clapham Common, he had noted a large number of footprints around the deceased, presumably left by the killer. He now had to admit to the court that no casts of these prints had been taken.

Inspector Wensley testified that no mention of a murder charge was made to Morrison when he was arrested. After spending some time in the cells, Morrison said that he wished to see the inspector. When he was taken through to the interview room, Morrison began by saying: 'I see you have accused me of a serious crime – you have accused me of murder.' It had, therefore, been Morrison who first mentioned murder.

Sergeant Brogden also confirmed that no mention of murder had been made and the name of Leon Beron had not been mentioned. Brogden also said that when Morrison was first seen in the café, Inspector Wensley had said: 'Stein, I want you.' He had not said: 'Stein, I want you for murder.'

Other police officers had been present at various times during the arrest process and all swore that no mention of a murder charge had been made. Thus, Detective Sergeant Henry Dessent, Constable Charles Staff, Inspector Roderick Mckenzie and Detective Sergeant Richard Nursey all gave evidence to that effect.

The only other important witness for the prosecution was Dr Frederick Freyberger, who had performed the post-mortem on Beron. He described four scalp wounds and five further wounds upon the forehead. All had been inflicted by means of some blunt metallic instrument. There were five cuts on the left side of Beron's face and two more on the right. These had been caused by a knife, as had three stab wounds on the body. All the stab wounds had apparently been caused soon after death, as there had been little bleeding from these wounds. The cause of death was fracture of the skull and concussion of the brain.

This, then, was the sum of the prosecution case. Morrison and Beron had been seen together on the night of the murder; Morrison had changed some sovereign coins, similar to those which Beron had been known to carry and Morrison had known that he was wanted for murder before that charge had been mentioned to him. It was now time for the defence to put their case.

The first defence witness was John Holmes Greaves, a surveyor, of 17 Old Burlington Street. At the request of the defence team he had visited Morrison's lodgings in Newark Street and examined the premises. He testified that once the door was locked by sliding the bolt across, it could only be opened by pulling the bolt back which was only done with a great deal of noise. Further, the window of Morrison's room was shaky and stiff and could again only be opened with a good deal of noise. In short, once the house was locked up for the night, Morrison could only have left if he roused the entire household. This testimony was important because of what the next two witnesses were to say.

Annie Zimmerman was Morrison's landlady at Newark Street. She told the court the she and her husband only ever retired for the night once the lodger had come in. That time varied but was seldom later than 11.00pm and very occasionally, as late as midnight. On New Year's Eve, Morrison had come in just before midnight and immediately went to bed. Annie's husband then locked up for the night and the house was not disturbed by anyone leaving. Morrison remained inside the house until 10.15am the next day.

This testimony was confirmed by Maurice Zimmerman, Annie's husband. He also told the court that the room he and Annie slept in was next to Morrison's and he would certainly have heard the prisoner had he left that house again that night.

Esther Grose lived next door to the Zimmermans at number 93 Newark Street. She was standing at her front door at close to midnight on 31 December and saw Morrison let himself in. Some five minutes later, Esher heard the bolt being drawn next door. She did not go to bed until 2.00am and heard no-one leaving number 91 during the night.

Esther Brodsky lived at 71 Cleveland Street and on New Year's Eve she had gone, with her sister Jane, to the Shoreditch Empire.

She knew Morrison and saw him sitting three or four seats away, in the same row. The show ended between 11.15am and 11.30pm and when Esther and Jane left, they saw Morrison standing in the doorway. He then walked them home. This evidence was confirmed by sixteen-year-old Jane Brodsky.

Michael Goldberg, a salesman, said that he had sold, amongst other items, half a dozen collars to Morrison. The bloodstained collar, which Morrison had been wearing when he was arrested, was identical to those collars. This sale took place on 4 January, three days after Beron had been murdered.

Florrie Delton, with whom Morrison had lived briefly in early January, testified that during his stay with her, Morrison's nose had started to bleed one day. This tendency to sudden nose bleeds was even confirmed by a prisoner warder: Herbert Raggett, of Brixton prison. He had seen Morrison's nose bleed for three or four minutes on 28 February.

Another warden from Brixton, William Cunningham, had also seen Morrison's nose bleed for no apparent reason. This occurrence had taken place on 15 February and was reported to the medical officer.

Perhaps the most important witness for the defence was Steinie Morrison himself. His testimony lasted for more than two days and he began by outlining where he had obtained his money from. He had traded in cheap jewellery and, at the end of November, had received £20 from his mother who lived in Russia. Then, in December, he had won £25 playing faro in a club in Greenfield Street.

Turning to the night of the murder of Leon Beron, Morrison said that he had been in the restaurant at around 8.00pm when he had sold some of his jewellery. From there he had gone to the Shoreditch Empire and after walking the two sisters home, had briefly returned to the restaurant. He did see Beron there but they did not speak or sit together. Morrison left the restaurant at 11.45pm and went straight back to his lodgings where he stayed the night.

Morrison was, though, an appalling witness and told lie after lie. He claimed that he had been born in Australia when it was easily shown that he was Russian. Also, he did not mention that much of the money he had suddenly come into had actually come from a Treasury Bill forgery he had taken part in with others. On 30 November, a forged bill for £300 had been passed at the Holloway branch of the London and South Western Bank. By not admitting his part in that crime, and thus avoiding a fraud charge, Morrison was risking putting his own neck into the noose on a much more serious one.

There were other minor witnesses for the defence. Lewis Minchinsky was Sam Rosen's landlord and he testified that on the night of the murder, Rosen was at home and in bed by 11.30pm so could not have seen Morrison with Beron as he had claimed.

Finally, Constable George Greaves was called to say that he was in the charge room at Leman Street police station when Morrison was brought in. He had demanded to know why he was there and Sergeant Brogden replied: 'I told you before, you are brought here on a serious charge – on suspicion of murder.' This showed that at least one police witness, Brogden, had certainly lied and, by

Mister Justice Darling who sentenced Steinie Morrison to death.
Author's collection

implication, so had all the others who had been present and claimed not to have heard the word murder being mentioned.

The jury deliberated for just thirty-five minutes before returning to announce that they had found Morrison guilty of murder. He was then sentenced to death but as the judge intoned the words: '...and may the Lord have mercy', Morrison interrupted with: 'I decline such mercy. I do not believe there is a God in Heaven either.' He was then taken to the condemned cell at Wandsworth prison to await his fate.

An appeal was entered and heard on 27 March, the defence concentrating on the evidence given by the three cabmen and asking that it be ruled inadmissible as all three had seen pictures of Morrison before making their identification. The judges ruled that there was enough evidence to convict, even without that testimony. The death sentence was confirmed.

In the event, Steinie Morrison did not hang. The Home Secretary, Winston Churchill, announced that he had advised His Majesty to commute the sentence to one of life imprisonment and Morrison was moved from Wandsworth to Dartmoor prison.

Morrison continued to maintain his innocence and began bombarding anyone and everyone with letters, asking for help to launch a new appeal. He went on hunger strikes to highlight his cause and even began to demand that his original death sentence be reinstated as he would rather face the noose than years in prison for a crime he had not committed.

In due course, public opinion began to swing behind Morrison and, by 1913, a petition for the case to be looked at again had gathered 42,000 signatures. It had no effect and Morrison continued with his routine of letters, hunger strikes and acts of violence against the system which had imprisoned him.

The years passed and still Morrison continued his campaign without respite. Such efforts could only ever have a detrimental effect upon his health and, at 2.15pm on 21 January 1921, Morrison suffered a heart attack. Despite prompt medical attention, he died that same day, at 4.30pm. A man who was almost certainly innocent, had been in custody, constantly protesting that innocence, for ten long years.

Chapter 4

Frederick Henry Seddon
1911-12

Tragic circumstances had caused Eliza Mary Barrow to have a number of different addresses in and around London.

Born on 23 November 1862, Eliza suffered three consecutive years of personal loss. In 1874, her father William Joseph Barrow died. The following year, 1875, her fourteen-year-old brother fell ill and died; and the year after that, 1876, her mother, also Eliza, passed away. Eliza was sent to live with relatives but at least her father had left her comfortably off. The problem was that, possibly through all this tragedy, Eliza had become rather difficult to live with and was subject to mood swings and fits of temper.

By 1896, Eliza, who was now thirty-four years old, was living with an aunt, Mrs Susannah Hook in Edmonton. When Mrs Hook died, in 1902, Eliza lodged with Mrs Grant, Mrs Hook's daughter, and Eliza's cousin, at 43 Roderick Road, Hampstead.

In November 1908, Mrs Grant also died and Miss Barrow briefly went to live with Mr and Mrs Kemp at 53 Wolsley Avenue. In fact, Eliza was no longer alone because Mrs Grant had had two children: Hilda and Ernest. Hilda was put into a children's home but Eliza took Ernest with her when she moved in with another cousin, Frank Vonderahe at 31 Eversholt Road, where she remained until July 1910.

In addition to Ernest, Eliza also took Ernest's uncle, Robert Ernest Hook, an ex-sweetheart of hers, and his wife and that extended family lived reasonably happily until a disagreement about food led Eliza to declare that she intended finding fresh lodgings for herself. So it was that on 26 July 1910, Eliza and Ernest Grant, along with Robert Hook and his wife, moved into 63 Tollington Park, the home of Frederick Henry Seddon, and his wife, Margaret Ann.

This new arrangement did not, however, last very long. A couple of weeks after moving in with the Seddons, in mid-August 1910, Eliza Barrow argued with Robert Hook. He had apparently taken his wife and Ernest out for the day and not asked her to join them. Angered by this, Eliza spoke to her new landlord and asked him to get the Hooks to leave the house. It was 10.00pm by the time Margaret Seddon, Frederick's daughter, handed Mr Hook a note, signed by Eliza, asking him and his wife to leave.

This seemed to cause a disagreement between Robert Hook and Frederick Seddon, perhaps because Hook might have been jealous of the influence Seddon appeared to have. Seddon had mentioned that Miss Barrow had now put all her affairs in his hands. Hook demanded if he meant all her money to which Seddon replied 'No'. Hook then made the somewhat surprising observation that he would defy Seddon and a regiment like him before he got hold of Eliza's money. This did nothing to calm the situation and at 1.30am the next morning, Seddon knocked on Hook's bedroom door and ordered that him and his wife to leave the house within twenty-four hours. He had even tacked a note to the door, containing a message to that effect, signed 'F Seddon. Landlord and Owner.' The couple duly moved out at 10.00am that same morning leaving Eliza Barrow and Ernest Grant behind, living on the top floor of the house.

Approximately one year later, at 8.20pm on Wednesday, 20 September 1911, Eliza's cousin, Frank Vonderahe called at 63 Tollington Park. His knock was answered promptly by Mary Chater, a servant of the household. Mr Vonderahe introduced himself and asked if he might see Miss Barrow.

'Don't you know she is dead and buried?' replied Mary. A shocked Vonderahe replied that he knew nothing of this and asked when the tragic event had taken place. Mary replied that she had been buried the previous Saturday 16 September and went on to say that Mr and Mrs Seddon were out but they would be back if he returned at 9.00pm.

Frank Vonderahe did indeed return at 9.00pm and this time his wife, Julia, accompanied him. Once again it was Mary Chater who opened the door but almost immediately, sixteen-year-old Margaret Seddon came to the door and apologised for the fact that her mother and father were still not home. They had gone to see a show at the Empire Theatre and probably wouldn't be home until quite late. Mr and Mrs Vonderahe decided that it would be best to leave their enquiries until the following day.

In fact, work commitments meant that Frank Vonderahe was unable to return to Tollington Park the next day. So it was that his wife, Julia and her sister-in-law, Amelia Blanche Vonderahe went to see Seddon. This time he was at home and greeted them in a civil and friendly manner.

After some discussion, Seddon explained that Miss Barrow had died on Thursday 14 September, after a long illness. She had, as Mary Chater had said, been buried two days later on, 16 September. The Vonderahe ladies were fully aware that Eliza had been a woman of considerable property and asked about the provisions she had made in her will. Seddon was happy to show them a copy of the will, signed in pencil, leaving all her property to be equally divided between Ernest Grant and his sister, Hilda. The two ladies were only satisfied for a few minutes, though, for Seddon went on to say that there was actually very little property left to dispose of. He then explained that Eliza had sold the vast majority of her property in order to purchase an annuity for herself. In summary, she had sold most of what she had in order to buy herself a regular income for as long as she lived. Now that she was dead, of course, that annuity had died with her.

'Whoever persuaded her to do that was a remarkably clever person' commented Amelia, but Seddon made no reply to this. Julia then asked him why the family had not been informed of the death whereupon Seddon produced a copy of a letter which he said had been sent to Eversholt Road. The letter was dated 14 September and read:

Dear Sir, I sincerely regret to inform you of the death of your cousin, Miss Eliza Mary Barrow, at 6.00am this morning, from epidemic diarrhoea. The funeral will take place on Saturday at about 1.00pm to 2.00pm.

Please inform Albert Edward and Emma Marion Vonderahe of her demise and let me know if you or they wish to attend the funeral.

I must also inform you that she made a will on the 11th instant, leaving what she died possessed of to Hilda and Ernest Grant and appointed myself as sole executor under the will.

Julia and Amelia were far from satisfied with what they had heard and returned home to tell their respective husbands what they had discovered. The two families discussed the matter and a decision as to what to do was finally made. Thus, on Monday 9 October, Frank Vonderahe visited Seddon's home again. This time a family friend, Mr Thomas Walker, went with him.

Mr Vonderahe began by asking to see the copy of the will for himself. This time Seddon was not as accommodating and immediately went onto the defensive by saying: 'You are not the eldest of the family, and I don't know whether I shall show it to you. Everything is perfectly legal and Miss Barrow did everything by herself.'

Trying a somewhat different approach, Frank Vonderahe then asked about specific properties he knew that his cousin had owned. One of these was a public house named the *Buck's Head* and Seddon replied that he now owned the lease on that establishment. He went on to say that he now also owned the lease on the barber's shop next door, and all the rest of the properties Eliza had owned. He also explained that all this property had been signed over for a total annuity of £3 per week.

There was little further action that Frank Vonderahe could take so, for the time being at least, the matter was allowed to rest there. The family were still far from satisfied and believed that the matter of Eliza's death and her financial dealings in the last year of her life deserved further investigation. Since there was nothing the family themselves could do, Frank sent a letter to the Director of Public Prosecutions, asking that he look into the matter. That letter was, as a matter of routine, passed on to the police. Having checked out the basic details of the story themselves, the police soon concluded that a closer look into the matter was indeed required.

On 15 November, Eliza Barrow's body was exhumed, and a post-mortem was then performed by Bernard Spilsbury, the pathologist. He removed and examined various internal organs and handed these to his colleague, Dr William Henry Willcox who then carried out a scientific analysis. The results of these tests and examinations showed that Miss Barrow had actually died from arsenical poisoning.

Of course, anyone inside the house at Tollington Park might have responsible for administering the poison. As the investigation proceeded it became clear that the maid, Mary Elizabeth Ellen Chater had very rarely given food to Miss Barrow. The same could be said of the daughter of the house, Margaret Seddon. Added to these considerations, there was also the fact that Frederick Seddon had, apparently, appropriated all of Miss Barrow's property, which surely gave him a motive. That was why Chief Inspector Alfred Ward stood outside 63 Tollington Park, on 4 December, waiting to arrest Frederick Henry Seddon.

It was 7.00pm when Ward finally saw Seddon approaching the house. The inspector identified himself and informed Seddon that he was to be arrested on suspicion of murder. Seddon replied: 'Absurd. What a terrible charge, wilful murder. It is the first of our family that has ever been accused of such a crime. Are you going to arrest my wife as well? If not, I would like you to give her a message for me.'

Once Seddon was in custody, the investigation continued and officers discovered that most of Eliza Barrow's food had actually been prepared by thirty-four-year-old Margaret Ann Seddon. It was now felt that she too might have been involved in the murder so, on 15 January 1912, she was also arrested and charged.

The joint trial of Frederick Henry Seddon and his wife, Margaret Ann, opened at the Old Bailey, before Mister Justice Bucknill, on 4 March. The proceedings would last until 14 March during which time the prosecution case was detailed by the Attorney-General, Sir Rufus D Isaacs, assisted by Mr Richard D Muir, Mr S A T Rowlatt and Mr Travers Humphreys. Frederick Seddon's defence was led by Mr Edward Marshall Hall, assisted by Mr J Wellesley Orr and Mr R Dunstan. Meanwhile, his wife

SEDDON'S WIDOW TELLS HOW MISS BARROW WAS POISONED.

"I SAW HIM GIVE THE POISON."

WHY SHE KEPT SILENT.

FULL STORY OF THE MURDER.

REMARKABLE CONFESSION.

[COPYRIGHT.]

On April 18 of this year FREDERICK HENRY SEDDON was hanged at Pentonville Gaol for the murder of Miss Barrow, an elderly and wealthy lady, who met her death at his hands by poison at his house at Tollington Park, North London.

To-day *The Weekly Dispatch* presents to its readers for the first time the true story of the crime, narrated by the widow. It is a striking and a pathetic document.

Mrs. Seddon (she has recently married again and is now Mrs. Cameron, but she will be best remembered by the name of Seddon) has been moved to tell the truth about the tragedy, owing to the cruel charges, veiled and anonymous, which are again being levelled against her.

As will be remembered, Mrs. Seddon was tried at the Old Bailey together with her late husband on the charge of murder, and she was acquitted. Thousands of people were of opinion at the time that she knew more about the tragedy than she disclosed at the trial, despite her protestations of innocence, and there

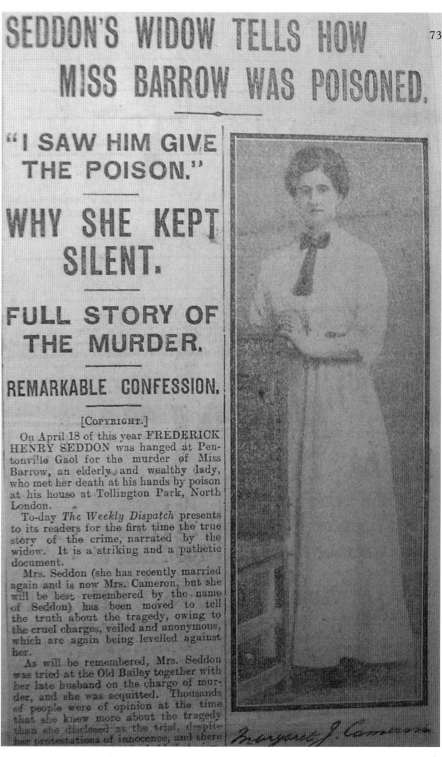

Margaret J. Cameron

The new Mrs Cameron – previously Margaret Ann Seddon, who stood trial with her husband for the murder of Eliza Barrow. This picture is from the article she penned after her husband had been executed. Author's collection

Margaret Ann, was defended by Mr Gervais Rentoul.

The first witness was Robert Ernest Hook, who began by detailing some of Eliza Barrow's history. He then went on to discuss some of the money he knew she had had in her possession. In October 1906, he had helped her count gold coins into a number of money bags and testified that altogether there had been £420. There was also a number of banknotes and all this money was then placed into a cashbox. That same cashbox had been seen by Hook at Tollington Park.

Hook was followed into the witness box by Frank Ernest Vonderahe, Eliza Barrow's cousin. He confirmed that whilst she was alive, Eliza had some rather peculiar habits and had dressed rather poorly for a woman of means. He too referred to some of the property and assets he knew his cousin had owned. In addition to the public house, which brought her in a rent of £105 per annum, there was the barber's shop next door which brought another £50. Eliza had also owned £1600 of three-and-a-half percent India Stock and had something like £200 in the Finsbury Savings Bank.

Frank had never received the letter, which Seddon said he had sent, informing him of Eliza's death. He told the court that he had moved from 31 Eversholt Road to 160 Corbyn Street in June, 1911. More importantly perhaps, he confirmed that he had never visited his cousin at Tollington Park from the date she first moved in, 26 July 1910, until the day he had called to speak to her and been informed of her death, 20 September 1911. He said that he had called on that day because he had had some information about his cousin, implying that he had heard that she had at least been ill. He gave no explanation as to why he had not called to visit her previously, in fourteen months, despite living close by.

Frank continued his testimony by talking about a letter he had received from Seddon, and dated 21 September. This began: 'To the relatives of the late Miss Eliza Mary Barrow, who died September 14th inst, at the above address, from epidemic diarrhoea, certified by Dr Sworn, 5 Highbury Crescent. Duration of illness, ten days.

'As executor under the will of Miss Barrow, dated September 11th 1911, I hereby certify that Miss Barrow has left all she died possessed of to Hilda and Ernest Grant, and appointed me as sole executor in trust until they become of age.

'Her property and investments she disposed of, through solicitors and stockbrockers, about October 1910 last, to purchase a life annuity, which she received monthly up to the time of her death. The annuity died with her. She stated in writing that she did not wish any of her relatives to receive any benefit at her death.'

Under cross-examination from Mr Marshall Hall, Vonderahe had to admit that Eliza had not got on with his family. On one occasion, Eliza had spat in his wife's face. He also confirmed that after the last Budget she had been concerned about her finances and had spoken to him about her worries over the *Buck's Head* public house. Further, Eliza was indeed the kind of woman who might well leave her property to a perfect stranger, on a whim.

Frank was followed into the witness box by his wife, Julia. She spoke of her visits to 63 Tollington Park and claimed that she had always been on friendly terms with Miss Barrow, skating over the incident where she had spat in her face and claiming that she had simply ignored it, as Eliza was in one of her moods. She also explained that the delay in her husband returning to Seddon's house was due to Seddon being away for a fortnight. He had mentioned this to Julia when she called on 21 September.

Amelia Vonderahe confirmed much of Julia's testimony. After a number of minor witnesses had then been called, Mr William Dell took the stand. He had moved in to 31 Eversholt Road on 1 September 1911, after the Vonderahes had left. Three days later, on 4 September, a circular had arrived for Mr Vonderahe so his son wrote 'not known' upon it and returned it. No further letters for the Vonderahes were ever delivered. This was confirmed by William's wife, Eleanor and his son, Stanley George Dell.

A series of witnesses followed all of whom proved that a series of banknotes, paid to Miss Barrow, had been processed through the hands of either of the prisoners. At this time, when an individual changed a banknote, they were asked to endorse it on the back. In all, six £5 notes had gone through Frederick Seddon's bank account and nine more had been endorsed on the back in the name of Scott, giving the address of Eversholt Road. These endorsements were in Margaret Seddon's handwriting. The notes covered the period 14 October 1910 to 21 August 1911. The final financial witnesses testified that in October 1910, Miss Barrow had transferred her India Stock to Frederick Seddon and, on 25 January 1911, he had sold that stock for the sum of £1519 16s 0d.

What had happened to that money? The next witness, Arthur Douglas Laing, was a clerk at the Lothbury branch of the London County and Westminster Bank. He told the court that on 25 January 1911, Frederick Seddon had opened a deposit account with a cheque for £1519 16s 0d. There had been just two withdrawals since that date. The first, for £119 16s, took place on 1 February 1911, leaving a balance of £1400. That full amount had then been drawn on 6 March, and the account closed.

Edwin Russell was a solicitor with offices at 59 Coleman Street. He said he had acted for Mr Seddon in the transfer of the lease of the Buck's Head and the barber's shop. The assignment was dated 11 January 1911 and in return, Seddon agreed to pay Miss Barrow £52 per annum, to be paid in monthly instalments. Under cross-examination from Mr Marshall Hall, Mr Russell agreed that his firm had, during the period of negotiation, received several letters from Miss Barrow and she had taken a keen and intelligent interest in the transfer.

Henry W Knight was another solicitor, working for Mr Russell's firm and he testified that he had acted for Miss Barrow in the matter of the transfer. He had taken the document to Miss Barrow for her perusal and read it to her. He especially recalled it as she was very deaf. She then read through the document herself and signed it in his presence

John Charles Pepper was the chief clerk at the Finsbury and City of London Bank. As early as 17 October 1887, Eliza Barrow had opened an account with his bank and on 19 June 1911, it had a credit balance of £216 9s 7d. On that date, Miss Barrow came into the bank with another lady and closed the account, taking the balance in cash. Mr Pepper was also able to confirm that at the time, there had been a run on the Birkbeck Bank, so large withdrawals were not uncommon.

The next witness was ten-year-old Ernest Grant who said that he known Miss Barrow all his life and used to call her 'Chicky'. Continuing his evidence, Ernest said that whilst at the Seddon's he had first of all slept with Miss Barrow but, later had had a room to himself. He recalled that he had gone on a holiday to Southend, and when he returned, found that she had fallen ill, and he began to sleep in the same room as her again.

On the last night Ernest had slept with Miss Barrow, she had been very ill and kept waking him up and asking him to call for Mrs Seddon. This happened several times during the night and eventually a very tired Ernest was put to bed in another room whilst both Mr and Mrs Seddon took care of Miss Barrow. He had never seen Chicky again.

The next day, Ernest and two of the Seddon children went to Southend again and stayed with a Mrs Jeffreys. It was there that he was first informed that Miss Barrow had died. Ernest then went on to confirm some of the arrangements at Seddon's house.

He recalled Mary Chater, the maid and said that she had never waited on Miss Barrow. Further, before Miss Barrow had fallen ill, she and Ernest used to always have their meals together and it was the Seddon's daughter, Margaret, who did most of the cooking. Once Miss Barrow was ill, however, all the meals were prepared by Mrs Seddon. Medicine had been prescribed for the illness and it was also Mrs Seddon who administered this.

Ernest too was cross-examined by Mr Marshall Hall and said that the Seddons were always very kind to Miss Barrow and that she was very fond of them. He also said that he personally was much happier living with the Seddons than he had been when they lived with the Vonderahes.

The two trips to Southend were then confirmed by two different ladies. Leah Jeffreys stated that the Seddons had come to stay with her from 8 August until 1 September 1911. They returned on 22 September, and stayed until 8 October. During that time Ernest Grant visited several times.

Annie Henderson of Riviera Drive, Southchurch, near Southend said that two of the Seddon children and Ernest Grant had stayed with her from 14 September until 28 September.

The next witness was the maid at Tollington Park, Mary Elizabeth Ellen Chater. She testified that she had worked for the Seddons, as a general servant, for approximately one year. She confirmed that it was Mrs Seddon who did all the cooking in the house and that her eldest daughter helped her prepare the food for Miss Barrow and Ernest Grant. Miss Barrow had also gone to Southend for a short time and had fallen ill when she returned. Mary was also able to say that Miss Barrow had suffered from diarrhoea and sickness before she had fallen seriously ill.

William Seddon was Frederick's father and had also been living at 63 Tollington Park. He confirmed that he had acted as a witness when Eliza Barrow signed her will on 11 September. It had been William who read it out to her and she had then asked for her glasses and read it herself. Finally, before she signed it she said: 'Thank God, that will do.'

Carl Taylor was the assistant superintendent for the Holloway District of the London and Manchester Industrial Assurance Company. Seddon was the superintendent and therefore Taylor's immediate superior. Each Thursday, Taylor would attend at 63 Tollington Park, where Seddon had an office in the cellar, to make up the accounts for the week.

On 14 September, Taylor arrived at 12.30pm. Seddon did not appear until one hour later and the two men then worked together through the afternoon. He seemed to be very tired and told Taylor that he had been kept up much of the previous night.

At around 9.00pm, Taylor heard the chink of money and turning, saw piles of gold coin on Seddon's desk. Taylor estimated that there was at least £200. As Taylor watched, Seddon packed the coins into four bags and put one of them in front of John Smith, another employee of the company, and joked, 'Here's your wages.' This encounter was then confirmed by the next witness, John Charles Arthur Smith.

Alfred Hartwell was a director of the assurance company and he stated that Seddon had been in his company's employ since 1891. Ten years after this, in 1901, he had been appointed as superintendent and in March of 1911, his salary was £5 5s per week. This rose by one shilling on 25 March.

The next important witness was William Nodes, the undertaker who had dealt with Miss Barrow's funeral. Mr Seddon had called on him at 11.30am on 14 September, said that a death had occurred at his house and he wished to arrange a funeral. He stressed that it must be an inexpensive one. They haggled a little over the price, with Nodes originally asking for £4 but eventually agreeing to a fee of £3 7s 6d.

If arsenic had been deliberately administered to Eliza Barrow then it had to have come from somewhere. A brand of flypapers, named Mather's, had been found at the house and the prosecution now called Walter Thorley, a chemist of 27 Crouch Hill.

Thorley stated that on 26 August 1911 a young girl had come to his shop, asking about flypapers. Thorley had since positively identified this girl as Seddon's daughter, Margaret and she had purchased a 3d packet containing six Mather's papers. These were of a type that needed to be soaked in water in order to make them effective. Questioned by Mr Marshall Hall, Thorley also admitted that Margaret was a friend of his daughter's and had called at the shop twice to see her. Margaret Seddon had been asked about this matter and denied ever purchasing the flypapers.

The time came for the various medical witnesses to give their testimony. The first of these was Dr John Frederick Paull who had first seen Miss Barrow in November 1910 when she attended his surgery complaining of feeling congested. On 1 August 1911, she came again, this time with Mrs Seddon and complained of the same ailment, and also said she was constipated. She was given a mixture of bicarbonate of soda and carbonate of magnesia.

Two days later, she returned, with Ernest Grant and then made further visits on 17 August and 22 August. Now the complaint was one of asthma and Dr Paull prescribed bicarbonate of potash and nux vomica.

Miss Barrow came again on 27 August and was given some chloral hydrate but she was back again on 30 August. During all of these visits she never complained of diarrhoea, sickness or pain. Finally, on 2 September, between 6.30pm and 8.00pm, Mrs

Seddon called and asked Dr Paull to visit the house in order to attend to Miss Barrow. The doctor refused to go.

Dr Henry George Sworn was the Seddon family doctor and had been since around 1902. On 2 September, as a result of a telephone call, he went to 63 Tollington Park where he saw Miss Barrow. Mrs Seddon was present and said that Miss Barrow had been ailing on and off for some time and was now suffering from sickness and diarrhoea. Dr Sworn's examination of the patient showed that she also had some abdominal pain for which he prescribed bismuth and morphia.

On 3 September, Dr Sworn called again and found Miss Barrow's condition unchanged. Things were the same on the 4th and Mrs Seddon told him that Miss Barrow had refused to take the medicine. He then told his patient that if she didn't take it, he would admit her to hospital.

Further visits followed on 7 September, and also the 8th and the 9th and it appeared that she was slowly improving. Dr Sworn next called on 11 September and she was still improving but was rather weak. The doctor said she should take Valentine's Meat Juice to build up her strength. Dr Sworn said he knew nothing about the making of a will around this time but was quite certain that she was quite capable of understanding what such a thing meant. She was in no way mentally affected.

On the morning of 13 September, Dr Sworn saw Miss Barrow again. Her condition had worsened and the sickness and diarrhoea was back. The following morning Mr Seddon came to Dr Sworn's house and said she had died at around 6.00am. Dr Sworn had no hesitation in giving a death certificate giving the cause of death as epidemic diarrhoea and exhaustion.

After Chief Inspector Ward had given his evidence, the prosecution called the pathologist, Bernard Henry Spilsbury. Spilsbury had performed the post-mortem on Eliza Barrow, after her exhumation, and had found no disease that would account for her death, though he did mention that her stomach and intestines were discoloured. Spilsbury had been present when Dr Willcox had conducted various tests for arsenic and as a result, Spilsbury had concluded that death was due to arsenic poisoning. Further, he was of the opinion that this was due to one or more large doses, rather than small doses over a long period of time.

Again, Spilsbury was cross-examined, this time by Mr Dunstan, and agreed that the red colouration he had found in the intestines, along with the absence of disease elsewhere, was equally consistent with death from epidemic diarrhoea extending over a period of from ten to twelve days. He also agreed that epidemic diarrhoea had been very prevalent in the previous September.

Spilsbury had referred to Dr Willcox and the prosecution now called Dr William Henry Willcox, the Senior Scientific Analyst to the Home Office. He had been present at the post-mortem and had obtained samples from the liver, stomach, intestines, spleen, kidneys, lungs and heart. He had also taken some bloodstained fluid from the chest, a portion of the brain, a muscle and some bone. On 29 November, Willcox had taken yet more samples, including some hair, more muscle and nails from the hands and feet. All of these samples were subjected to tests and large amounts of arsenic were discovered in the stomach, intestines, liver and muscles. He also found traces of arsenic in the hair and nails.

Dr Willcox then detailed the precise findings he had made. In the stomach he had found 0.11 grains of arsenic. In the intestines was 0.63 grains but the total amount found throughout the body was 2.01 grains. This in turn led to the deduction that a dose of up to five grains had been taken within three days of death.

An interesting experiment had been conducted by Dr Willcox. He had obtained some of the Mather's flypapers for testing and extracting the arsenic from them, in solution, by soaking them in water. He had also examined the solution made from Valentine's meat extract, which Eliza Barrow had been known to take in the days before her death. Willcox reported that the two solutions were identical in colour. Whilst the prosecution used this evidence to suggest that the arsenic could well have been administered in the Valentine's, the defence could claim that there was a possibility that Miss Barrow might have drunk the arsenic solution accidentally, mistaking it for Valentine's.

Another factor was that after Eliza's death, Seddon had taken some hair from her head and kept it in an envelope. This too had been sent for analysis and showed the presence of arsenic.

At that point, the case for the prosecution was closed and the defence barristers argued that there was not sufficient evidence to convict either of the prisoners. Mr Marshall Hall pointed out that there had been no evidence that either had purchased any of the flypapers or arsenic in any other form. There was also the fact that arsenic had been found in the hair showing that arsenic had been taken, probably in quite small doses, over a period of at least a year. The Marsh test, used to detect the presence of arsenic, would not suggest what quantities existed and the slightest error in any calculations performed to determine what dose might have been taken would greatly magnify the figures. Mr Rentoul, on behalf of Mrs Seddon, agreed with all this and asked that his client be discharged. Mister Justice Bucknill ruled that the case must proceed.

The first defence witness was Sydney Arthur Naylor who had known Frederick Seddon for about six years. He had visited 63 Tollington Park in the summer of 1909 and seen a bag of gold that must have contained at least £150. It appeared that the Seddons also carried on a business dealing in wardrobes and made a good deal of money from that venture.

The next witness was someone the entire court had waited to hear from; Frederick Seddon himself. His testimony lasted more than two full days. He began by giving some personal details including the fact that he had five children still living. Continuing, he said that he had run a wardrobe business, in his wife's name, and this had proved to be very profitable. He liked to keep a good deal of cash in hand, never less than £50 and often much more.

He had purchased 63 Tollington Park in August 1909 and at about the same time, he and his wife had had a disagreement on a family matter and parted for a short time. His original plan had been to convert the house into flats but, in January 1910, he was reconciled with his wife and they moved into the house with their children.

In July 1910, Seddon advertised some rooms to let and Miss Barrow called and agreed to take them at twelve shillings per week. In due course, Miss Barrow, Ernest Grant and Mr and Mrs

Hook moved in. Very soon there was some trouble and he asked Miss Barrow to move out. She said she wished to stay and added that the cause of the trouble was Mr Hook. The very next day, the Hooks took Ernest Grant out, leaving Miss Barrow behind. As a result, Miss Barrow wrote Hook a note, asking him to leave.

All of this trouble had greatly distressed Miss Barrow and at one stage she went down to the dining room, with a cash box, and asked Seddon if he would keep this in his safe. That was agreed and at no stage did Seddon examine the contents or know how much was inside.

The original agreement had been that Mr and Mrs Hook would live rent free at 63 Tollington Park on condition that they looked after Miss Barrow. Now that they were gone, someone else had to take care of her and that fell to Seddon's daughter, Margaret, who was then paid one shilling per day for her trouble.

In the autumn of 1910, Seddon's wife and daughter told him that Miss Barrow had been crying a lot and was very upset about her property. He then spoke to her and she told him that her main source of income was the rent from the *Buck's Head* public house. The recent budget had increased the taxation on licensed premises and she was concerned that this would reduce her income. There was also a barber's shop but much of the trade there came from the pub next door. They were dependent on each other and Miss Barrow thought that she might end up losing as much as £3 per week.

Next, Miss Barrow mentioned the India Stock. When she had purchased this, it had stood at 108 but was now down to 94. She went on to say that a friend of hers had purchased an annuity and she would like to do the same. Seddon reminded her that any annuity would die with her. She was unconcerned about that saying that she didn't want her relatives to have anything as they had all treated her so badly.

After much discussion, Seddon agreed to pay the annuity himself and the various transfers were made. Seddon then went on to detail what he had done with the money raised from the sale of the India Stock. Using £1400 of it, he had purchased fourteen leasehold houses.

Seddon now turned to the matter of flypapers. The summer of 1911 had been quite a hot one and consequently there were a large number of flies in the house. Miss Barrow complained about these so Seddon's wife obtained some flypapers for her. Seddon claimed never to have handled any of these and denied ever obtaining any solution or concoction from them.

After detailing the events on the night of Eliza Barrow's death, when she was in need of constant attention, Seddon said that he had written to the relatives to inform them of her death and did not know they had moved from Eversholt Road. He had asked his daughter to post it for him. Finally, he had taken a lock of hair from Miss Barrow to hand on to Ernest and Hilda Grant as a remembrance.

In his own evidence for the prosecution, Mr Hook had referred to the move from Eversholt Road to Tollington Park. On that occasion he claimed that he had Eliza Barrow's cash box and knew that it was full of gold. The defence now called Thomas Creek, a carman, who had helped in that move. He swore that although Hook helped him to load and unload the cart, he had not had anything in his hand as they made the journey.

The next witness was the other defendant, Margaret Ann Seddon. She confirmed much of what her husband had said. Turning to the flypapers, Margaret said that it was Miss Barrow herself who asked for them and specified that she did not want the sticky type but preferred the ones you soak. Margaret bought some for her on either 4 September or possibly the 5th, from a chemist named Meacher. She was not asked to sign the poisons book.

Turning to the day Miss Barrow died, Margaret said that at one stage her husband had asked if she knew where Miss Barrow's keys were. After a search, they were found in a drawer and her husband then opened the cash box in front of Margaret. It contained just £4 10s in gold in a little brown paper bag.

The Seddon's daughter, Margaret, was the next witness. She told the court that on 6 December, after her father had been arrested but before her mother was taken into custody, she was sent, by her mother, to purchase some flypapers from Price's

The Old Bailey where Seddon, and many of the others in this book, faced their trials for murder. Author's collection

chemists shop. That visit was made on the orders of Mr Saint, who was acting as her father's solicitor. She had only ever been to Thorley's shop to see his daughter and had never purchased flypapers from him.

Alice Rutt had worked two days per week for the Seddons, to do the housework and by coincidence, one of the days she called was the day of Miss Barrow's death. She had been present when Mr Seddon opened the cash box and confirmed that it only contained £4 10s.

Margaret Ann Seddon was then recalled to clear up the matter of her short separation from her husband at the time of the purchase of 63 Tollington Park. She confirmed that their disagreement was over a business matter. She left him on 3 January 1910 and returned to him after five weeks.

There the defence rested. The jury retired to consider their verdict and after an absence of one hour, returned to announce that they had found Margaret Seddon not guilty, but that Frederick Henry Seddon was guilty as charged. Margaret was then discharged and Frederick was asked if he had anything to say before sentence was passed.

Seddon made a very long speech which ended with a reference that he belonged to the same brotherhood as the learned judge:

Freemasonry. This did nothing to save Seddon from the only possible sentence allowed for murder, and Mister Justice Bucknill then sentenced him to death.

An appeal was entered on the grounds that there was no proof that it had been Seddon who administered the arsenic to Miss Barrow. That appeal was heard on 1 April before Justices Darling, Channell and Coleridge. On the second day, the three judges ruled that there was sufficient circumstantial evidence to show that he had killed her in order to steal her property and her gold; the sentence must stand.

On Thursday 18 April 1912, Frederick Henry Seddon, prisoner number 13990, was hanged at Pentonville by John Ellis and Thomas Pierrepoint. Before he died, he wrote one last letter to his wife in which he maintained again that he was innocent.

Before we examine the possibility of a miscarriage of justice, there is one more important factor to consider; something that had been missed in many previous accounts of this story.

On 17 November 1912, almost seven months to the day since Seddon had been hanged, an article appeared in the *Weekly Despatch*. It was an article in which Seddon's widow told her own story and it was headed: 'I saw Seddon poison Miss Barrow.'

The article began with Margaret confirming that she had remarried and was now Mrs James Cameron, and was living at 361 Price Street, Birkenhead. It went on to say that she was telling the truth now because many people still believed that she was involved in some way and now wished to clear her name.

According to Margaret's story, Seddon had carefully planned the murder and on the last night of Eliza Barrow's life, he had substituted a mixture made up of the water from the flypapers and a white powder, for Miss Barrow's medicine. He had then given this to her, whilst Margaret was present.

Her first instinct was to tell the police at once but he had then taken a revolver from his pocket and said he would blow her brains out if she informed on him. After his arrest, she still didn't inform on her husband because she held out the faint hope that he might be acquitted and thus his children would be spared the disgrace of being branded the offspring of a murderer.

Margaret then went on to blacken Seddon's character even further. She said that she was a native of Liverpool and that was where she had first met Seddon, when she was just fifteen. They had started walking out together but one night another man had said he wished to make her acquaintance. Seddon produced a revolver and said that he would kill anyone who came between them.

Despite this, their relationship continued and they eventually married. A few days after the ceremony Seddon thrashed her so hard that she was laid up in bed. She returned to her mother's house but went back to Seddon shortly afterwards. Some time later Seddon hit her so hard he knocked out her teeth and she took out a summons against him. A legal separation was drawn up but she forgave him yet again, even though every night, Seddon slept with a loaded revolver beneath his pillow.

Margaret confirmed that at Seddon's request, she had purchased four flypapers. Later, after Miss Barrow had died, Seddon ordered that the body be stripped as soon as possible and the room should be cold so that the doctor, when he called, would accept that she had died earlier.

If we take this article at face value, we are expected to believe that Margaret gave the interview in order to clear her own name of suspicion. Yet by this time she had moved halfway across the country, had remarried and now had a completely new name. We are also expected to believe that she stood in the dock at the Old Bailey, facing the possibility of death by hanging, in order to protect her children's names. How would this have protected them? Even if both defendants had been found not guilty, the stigma of suspicion would have remained, just as it did, in fact, with Margaret. Surely she would have told the police all that she knew the moment she was arrested in January.

Even more curious is that Margaret had been in contact with the press before. On 17 March 1912, a letter from her was published in *Lloyds Weekly News*. In this letter she stated that she firmly believed in her husband's innocence and referred to a conversation she had had with Frederick in the cells after he had been found guilty and sentenced to death. In this conversation her husband had said: 'Maggie, you know I am absolutely innocent of this dreadful charge. God is my judge. He knows. For goodness sake it is no use of you breaking down like this. You have the children to think of.'

'There is one thing. You must go down on your hands and knees and thank God that you are spared to look after the children. Bear up, because it will grieve me to know that you are worrying.'

How do we reconcile these two diametrically opposed articles? It simply does not make sense.

There are surely a number of possibilities here. One of those is that Frederick Seddon did indeed kill Miss Barrow in order to seize her property. Yet, when we look at this more carefully, it starts to make less sense.

Eliza Barrow moved into 63 Tollington Park on 26 July 1910. The transfer of her property; the public house, the barber's shop and the India Stock, took place on 11 January 1911. Seddon sold that same stock on 25 January 1911. In short, if Seddon were guilty of stealing that property then he had done so within six months of Eliza moving into his house. Why would he then need to kill her? It was agreed by the witnesses to the transfers and the various solicitors involved that Miss Barrow had made the transfers voluntarily and knew full well what she was doing. Even if the Vonderahes had later discovered what had happened, they could have done nothing about it. Added to this, of course, is that the Vonderahes were unlikely to find out as they never called at Tollington Park to see their relative, until after they received information that she was very ill.

The fact is that Seddon had no need to kill Eliza Barrow. If theft were his motive then he had achieved all he wished. He did have to pay out £52 per year under the annuity but that was a relatively small sum to him. We are expected to believe that having appropriated all her property, Seddon then waited a further eight months before killing her. We also have to consider that this cunning and intelligent man then kept a lock of his victim's hair knowing that it might well contain the arsenic he had administered.

Perhaps the killer was really his wife, Margaret. This is unlikely.

She had no real motive herself but how are we to explain her magazine article at the end of 1912? Is it not more likely that in order to deflect any blame from herself, she invented a story of a brutal husband who would stop at nothing to get what he wanted? Seddon was in no position to defend himself, and his name could hardly be blackened any further.

Could it be that the killer was actually Margaret, the daughter? Had she grown tired of looking after a demanding woman for one shilling per day? Again it hardly seems a likely motive.

There is one final answer. Perhaps Eliza Barrow killed herself, accidentally. We know that the flypaper soaked water was identical in colour to the meat extract. Could she have accidentally drunk down some of the poisonous liquid and died as a consequence? Added to this it must be remembered that Seddon had taken a lock of Eliza's hair after her death. This too had been subjected to chemical analysis and indicated that Eliza had apparently been imbibing arsenic over a prolonged period of time. Had she been taking it herself as a tonic? Alternatively, were the tests correct and was arsenical poisoning even the real cause of death?

There is more than one explanation for the death of Eliza Barrow. We know that she had financial concerns and entered into voluntary agreements to dispose of her property in return for an annuity. There is no evidence that she was manipulated by Seddon, or indeed anyone else and therefore there is doubt.

One must remember that in an English court, one does not have to prove innocence. It is for the prosecution to prove guilt beyond a reasonable doubt. In the case of Frederick Henry Seddon there is such a reasonable doubt and in consequence, he should not have been executed at Pentonville prison.

Chapter 5

Frederick Stephen Fuller
and James Murphy
1927

Henry Dennard and his brother William, two horse-dealers, were living in a caravan on Magdala Road, South Croydon. At approximately 8.30am on Sunday 15 May 1927, the two brothers were grazing their horses on Brancaster Lane, when something attracted their attention.

There was a fenced-off building site on Brancaster Lane and inside the compound was an office complex. There, lying on his side in front of this office, was an unconscious man.

The first thought of the brothers was that the man was drunk. They walked across to where he lay and tried to assist him to his feet but it was clear that he was unable to stand unaided. By now he did seem to be recovering some degree of consciousness and even tried to say something but it was really nothing more than an unintelligible mumble. The brothers gently lowered him back to the ground but realised that they couldn't just leave him there. Convinced by now that he was under the influence of alcohol the brothers thought that since the office door was open, it would be best to put him inside there, where at least he would be protected from the elements.

Going inside the office, the brothers saw a chair and placed the man onto it. As they left the office, they also noticed that his nose was slightly scratched. They assumed that he had grazed his nose when he had fallen to the ground outside.

Just as Henry and William were leaving the office, Henry Willis, a greengrocer of 57 Napier Road was passing the site. He noticed the two brothers, and no doubt wondering what they had been doing inside the office, called out and asked them what the problem was. Henry and William told him what they had found and Willis briefly went inside the office to see for himself. He saw the man, still in the chair and would later describe him as semiconscious. Willis too noticed the slight scratches around the man's nose.

Some four hours later, at 12.15pm, John Holden Ladd walked on to that same building site on Brancaster Lane. The door to the office was closed but when Ladd tried it, he found that it was unlocked. Going inside he found a man lying on his back, with his head resting on some rolls of wallpaper. There was blood on his right cheek and his nose was quite badly injured, either from a blow or possibly from falling onto it. Further, Ladd recognised the man immediately. He was the night-watchman on the site, forty two year old James Staunton. Ladd wasted no time in calling for the police and medical assistance.

The initial police investigation revealed that some coils of lead and some brass had been stolen from the site late on the night of Saturday 14 May, so it was natural to assume that the robbery and assault had been connected. The suggestion was that someone had broken into the site, been caught by Staunton and a scuffle had followed during which he had been badly hurt. Inquiries, therefore, concentrated on finding out who had stolen the metal.

Charles Henry Britton, who lived at 4 Sylverdale Road in Croydon had been walking out with his girlfriend on the evening of 14 May. As they passed the building site on Brancaster lane, Britton noticed a grey Ford van parked outside with a man standing at the rear of it. At first, Britton thought nothing of it, until he saw two other men come out of the yard, carrying coils of metal. Charles Britton had the foresight to take the number of the van: KX 871. That van was soon traced to three men: Joseph Torch, James Cornelius Pearson and Hedley Albert McCormack. These three were picked up and questioned and all three were charged with theft, on 19 May. Later still, on 29 June, Pearson and Torch would both receive sentences of six months imprisonment with hard labour for office breaking and theft, whilst McCormack was adjudged to be not guilty. The problem was that on the day of their initial arrest, it had become clear that these men had nothing to do with the attack upon James Staunton.

Other witnesses had come forward and they were able to piece together Staunton's movements on the night he had been attacked. John Ladd, the man who had found the unconscious man when he visited the site on the Sunday, had also been there at 7.00pm on 14 May. Staunton was at his post at that time.

By 8.30pm, Staunton was in the *Royal Oak* public house on Brighton Road, Purley, where he was served with three pints of beer. He was seen there by the barman, James Ambrose, and a number of other customers and they reported that he left at around 9.55pm. Ambrose was also able to state that when he did leave, Staunton had two pints of beer in bottles and a eighth of a pint of whisky which he took with him in a carrier bag.

Thomas Ferris was one of those other customers in the *Royal Oak,* and he actually left with Staunton and walked part of the way with him, towards Brancaster Lane. In due course, Ferris went off towards his own home at 34 Riddlesdown Road and at 10.05pm, he saw Staunton heading off alone, towards the building site.

These witnesses accounted for Staunton's whereabouts from 7.00pm on 14 May 1927, until just after 10.00pm. Charles Britton had seen the metal thieves at the yard, at around 9.45pm. That meant that the theft had taken place long before Staunton arrived back at the building site.

At 3.15pm on Tuesday 17 May, James Staunton died in the Memorial Hospital at Purley. As far as the police were concerned, this was now a case of murder and by now, the investigation had changed direction. One of the men who worked as a labourer on the site had not turned up for work on the Monday. There was nothing unusual in that since he was scheduled to have that day off anyway but when he also failed to appear on the Tuesday, the day Staunton died, alarm bells began to rang. This man was thirty-five-year-old Frederick Stephen Fuller, who lived at 33 Helder Street, South Croydon.

A quick check on Fuller revealed a rather unsavoury character. He had first come to the attention of the police in 1918 when he was arrested on a charge of having carnal knowledge with a girl aged below the age of sixteen. He had been a gunner in the Royal Garrison Artillery at the time and appeared to face the charge, at Guildford, on 2 September 1918. He was acquitted of the charge.

Four years later, on 6 January 1922, Fuller was sentenced to three months imprisonment by Croydon magistrates for common assault. After an argument he had struck two men in the face, with his fists, and then slashed them on the ear and neck with a razor.

A married man with six children already, two of which were in homes, his wife was now heavily pregnant with number seven. Added to this, his eldest daughter, now sixteen, had recently given birth to a child at the Mayday Road Hospital in Croydon. The baby had died aged just six days old and their were strong rumours in the district that Fuller was the father of that child.

Further checks showed that Fuller had a very close friend: James Murphy, and he too had a criminal record having served one months imprisonment with hard labour starting on 19 May 1925, for an assault on the police. Murphy too was a married man, living at 21 Napier Road with his wife and three children.

The police visited the homes of both Fuller and Murphy and found that both had not been home since the night of the attack upon James Staunton. Fuller's wife, Louisa May, was asked to contact the investigating officers immediately if she heard from her husband, and this she agreed to do.

The police did not have to wait for very long. On 22 May, Mrs Fuller received a letter from her husband which gave the return address of the *Bridge Hotel* in Doncaster. The following day, 23 May, both men were arrested and brought back to London for interview.

Fuller and Murphy readily admitted stealing money from Staunton. Fuller said that he had found Staunton lying on the floor and assumed that he was drunk. He had then rifled through his pockets, stolen what money he had on him, and then left him lying where he was. Murphy's own statement said much the same. The police were far from satisfied with these explanations and continued their questioning. Eventually both men made second statements in which they admitted striking Staunton but denied murder.

According to these new statements, Fuller and Murphy had gone to the building site for no particular reason. Staunton was there and demanded to know what they wanted. After some argument, Staunton offered to fight and Fuller hit him once with the back of his hand. Murphy had then come to his friend's aid and struck Staunton once on the jaw, knocking him out. Only then did they rifle through his pockets and take what money he had.

This statement raised an interesting point of law. If Fuller and Murphy had gone to the site with the express intention of stealing from Staunton, and in the process of doing so had caused him injuries which resulted in his death, then they were guilty of murder. If, however, the robbery had followed what was a fair fist fight, then they were guilty of manslaughter. That point could be the difference between life and death for the two prisoners. As far as the police were concerned, there was enough evidence to suggest that this was a case of murder and so both men were charged accordingly.

The trial of Fuller and Murphy took place at Guildford on 5 July 1927, before Mister Justice Rowlatt. Mr J D Cassels and Mr Moran appeared for the Crown whilst Mr C R Algar appeared for Fuller and Mr S Sueffert, represented Murphy.

The statements made by the two prisoners had detailed their movements after the attack upon Staunton and witnesses were now called to prove those movements.

Fuller and Murphy claimed that after leaving the building site they had walked to the *Royal Oak* public house from where they had caught a bus to the *Red Deer*. William Charles Burrage had seen both men on the way to the *Red Deer* at some time between 10.20pm and 10.30pm. The three men had fallen into conversation and after they had said they had no money, Burrage gave one of them twopence, though he was unable to say which man he had given it to.

After getting off the bus at the *Red Deer*, Fuller and Murphy said they had gone to the Ideal Tea Rooms, on Brighton Road. A number of witnesses recalled that visit.

Phyllis Irene Cooper was the waitress at the café and she recalled two men coming into her establishment, ordering cups of tea and staying for some ten minutes in total. She remembered them particularly because the men paid with a ten shilling note.

Three of the customers in the café; Benjamin John Osbourne, John Atkins and James Young, also remembered the two defendants coming into the tea room. Osborne had seen one of them change either a ten shilling or a one pound note; he could not be sure which. Atkins went a little further in his evidence saying that it was certainly a ten shilling note and it had been Murphy who handed it over.

In their statements, the two men had said that after leaving the café they had caught a bus to West Croydon from where they caught a train to London Bridge station, then walked about London for a while. By now the shops were opening and they called into a shop in Middlesex Street and purchased two new suits. This was confirmed by Mr Jack Valentine who ran a tailor's shop from 47-49 Middlesex Street.

The next witness, Henry Hughes, was an attendant in a gentleman's lavatory at Aldgate. He remembered seeing Fuller and Murphy come into the lavatory, go into cubicles and change their suits. After they had changed, one of the men asked Hughes what they could do with their old clothes and he told them to take them away with them.

The final part of the police statements showed that Fuller and Murphy had then caught the 10.55am train for Bradford. They stayed in that city until the morning of Tuesday, 17 May when they travelled to Leeds from where they then moved on to Doncaster and booked in at the *Bridge Hotel*. It had been from there that Fuller had written to his wife.

Medical evidence would be important in this case. The first doctor to give evidence was Dr Arthur Lancester who testified that he had first seen Staunton at the hospital at 2.00pm on Sunday 15 May. He had seen him again the following morning. Dr Lancester reported that his patient was suffering from a severe contusion at the back of his head. In Dr Lancester's opinion, that injury could only have been caused by either a fall from a height or from a direct blow to the back of the head.

Once Staunton had died from his injuries, the post-mortem was carried out by Dr Robert Matthew Bronte. He detailed all the injuries he had discovered. There was a four inch square haemorrhage over the left parietel and occipital bone. Abrasions were observed on Staunton's forehead, right cheek and nose. There was also bruising on each side of the chin and a bruise to the outer side of the left breast. Five further bruises were observed over the ribs and on the right upper arm. Finally, there was bruising over the left hip and on the inner side of the left shin. The direct cause of death had been bruising and haemorrhage to the back of the brain.

The jury faced a difficult decision but after much deliberation they came to the conclusion that Fuller and Murphy had gone to the site with the express purpose of robbing Staunton. The robbery had therefore come first, Staunton had been killed in pursuance of theft and therefore the two prisoners were guilty of murder. Mr Justice Rowlatt then sentenced both men to death.

Confirmation of the executions of Fuller and Murphy. The National Archives

Metropolitan Police.   No 728. (Unruled)   23 A

Reference to Papers

CROYDON STATION. " Z " DIVISION.

201/MR/924.

4th AUGUST 1927.

.1.

To Acting D.D.Inspector.

    With further reference to the attached:-

    I beg to report that at 11-30am on the 3rd, of August 1927, after the execution of Frederick Stephen Fuller and James Murphy, I attended H.M.Prison, Wandsworth, where an inquest was held by Samuel Ingleby Oddie Esq., Coroner.

    After I had given evidence of identification and Sir Bernard Spilsbury as to a post mortem examination he had made on the bodies, the Jury returned the usual verdict of "Death caused by hanging according to Law"

                                                        Sergt.
Humphrey Luckett.

ctg D.D.Inspector.

An appeal was entered, and this was heard on 18 July by the Lord Chief Justice, sitting with Justices Avory and Salter. Again the defence argument was that the robbery had come after a fair fight and the correct sentence was guilty of manslaughter. The judges did not agree and the appeal was duly dimissed.

Just over two weeks later, on Wednesday 3 August 1927, Frederick Stephen Fuller and James Murphy were hanged together at Wandsworth prison by Robert Baxter who had three assistants: Lionel Mann, Henry Pollard and Thomas Phillips. Whilst the two men had been awaiting their fate in the condemned cells, Mrs Fuller had given birth to their seventh child, a girl.

There are actually two grounds for considering that Fuller and Murphy should, after all, have been found guilty of manslaughter and thus spared the hangman's noose.

The first of these has already been mentioned; that the fight came before the robbery. Whilst it was true that both men had previous convictions for violence, neither had convictions for robbery or theft. Both men were the type who might let their fists do the talking for them but it seems within the bounds of probability that they were telling the truth, in that they assaulted Staunton after an argument and then decided to rob him. Neither scenario could be proved beyond doubt and, therefore, the defendants should have been given the benefit of the doubt.

The other factor was missed by the defence at the time. Stauton's semi-conscious form was seen by three men, Henry and William Dennard and also Henry Willis. All three reported that the only injuries they observed were some slight scratches or abrasions around Staunton's nose. They also agreed that when they left him in the office, at around 8.30am, he was sitting in a chair. By the time Staunton was seen again, by John Holden Ladd, at 12.15pm, he was lying on his back, there was blood on his cheek and his nose looked to be badly injured. More importantly, Staunton's head was resting on a number of rolls of wallpaper. In fact, there was a total of thirty-one rolls.

There is no suggestion that Staunton was the victim of a second attack. It seems obvious, therefore, that at some time in those intervening four hours, he slipped from the chair and landed heavily on the rolls of wallpaper. It is also likely that at that time he injured himself again, possibly then sustaining the injuries to the back of his head. It must be remembered that Ladd found Staunton lying on his back, which also lends weight to this argument. In addition, the various prosecution witnesses who had been inside that office all reported that the only blood they observed was on Staunton's neckerchief and the rolls of wallpaper.

If this is the case then it means that the injuries, which finally caused the death of James Staunton, were not inflicted by Fuller and Murphy and they should only have been found guilty of manslaughter.

Chapter 6

Harry Armstrong

1939

The year 1939 was a pivotal time in the history of the twentieth century. The last months of that period saw the start of one of the bloodiest wars of all, which plunged the world into six long years of terrible conflict. In England, however, 1939 began as a time of hope; that war might be avoided and peace would be maintained. Monday 2 January, was just another normal workday, now that the festivities of the New Year were over. That was certainly true for Kathleen Lawrence, a chambermaid at a hotel situated at 22 York Road, London. She was busily attending to the cleaning of the bedrooms, just as she did every other day. One of the rooms she was due to service was number 6, on the third floor.

Kathleen knocked gently on the door but there was no reply. She knew that the occupants of the room were the young couple who had checked in two days previously, on 31 December, but as far as she was aware, neither of them had gone out that morning. Kathleen knocked two or three times more but again there was no reply. Sighing to herself, Kathleen called for the hotel manager, Mr Richard Vaughan Jones who, by coincidence, was attending to something in the very next room.

Mr Jones knocked on the door of room 6 himself, his own hand being somewhat heavier than Miss Lawrence's, but he too received no reply. Somewhat wearily, Mr Jones then walked down to reception in order to pick up the pass key.

Finally gaining access to room 6, Jones saw that the light was still on. The male guest who had checked in, Mr Armstrong, was nowhere to be seen but his wife lay asleep in bed. Richard Jones crossed to the bed and gently tried to wake Mrs Armstrong but she did not stir. Then, as he pulled back the top blanket a little,

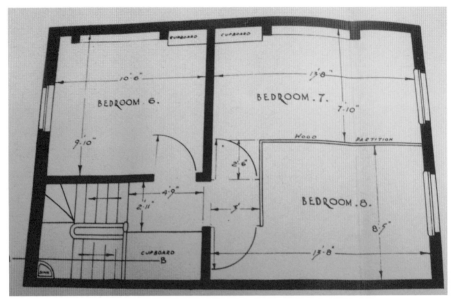

The layout of the rooms at the hotel where Irene Pentecost met her death. She was killed in room 6. The National Archives

Jones saw why he had not had the courtesy of a reply to his previous knocking. Some of the bedclothes had been forced into Mrs Armstrong's mouth and she was, quite obviously, dead. Jones wasted no time in sensibly locking the room again before dashing downstairs to telephone for the police.

A more detailed layout of room 6. The National Archives

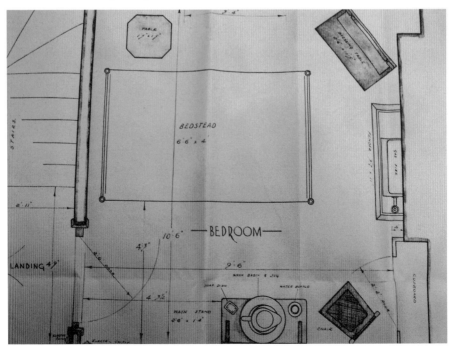

The first senior officer to arrive at the hotel was Detective Inspector William Fury. He thought it best not to touch the body until the pathologist arrived but did make a careful inspection of the room itself. Fury noticed an empty half-bottle of sherry and a glass tumbler on the bedside table. A sniff at the tumbler showed that it had indeed contained sherry at some stage. Fury also saw two suitcases and Richard Jones readily identified them as the ones Mr and Mrs Armstrong had carried with them when they checked in at some time between 8.30pm and 9.00pm on New Year's Eve, Saturday 31 December.

Inspector Fury asked Richard Jones what other information he might be able to furnish. Jones replied that when they had arrived, the young couple explained that they had married very recently and were then given room 8. They took their own luggage up to that room, having signed the register as Mr and Mrs Armstrong of Seaford in Sussex. Soon afterwards they had gone out for the night, presumably to join in the festivities, but they had returned by 10.00pm and retired for the night.

The next time Jones had seen Mr Armstrong was at 9.55am the following morning, New Year's Day. He did not see Mrs Armstrong but the couple must have gone out together at some stage for Jones saw them return together at 8.30pm. As they collected their key, Jones asked Mr Armstrong what time he and his wife wished to be called down for breakfast, adding that whilst they were out he had taken the liberty of moving their luggage to room 6, which was a better room.

Mrs Armstrong was already on her way up the stairs and her husband had to call up to her to ask her what time she wished to be called the next morning. After some discussion, Armstrong said that they wished to be called at 8.30am so that they might have breakfast at 9.00am. Armstrong then paid the bill for two nights and confirmed that they would be leaving after breakfast.

Before he had gone up to the room, Armstrong had asked Jones for a corkscrew. Mr Jones said that he did not really approve of drinking alcohol in the rooms but Armstrong replied that his wife had very recently been beset by family problems and, after all, they were celebrating the New Year. Somewhat reluctantly, Jones handed over the corkscrew.

Approximately one hour later, around 9.30pm or perhaps 9.45pm, Jones thought he might have seen Armstrong again, though he could not be sure. All he was certain of was that he had seen the back of a man as he entered the lavatory on the ground floor. The build of the figure was identical to Armstrong's, but Jones would not swear that it was he. Finally, at 11.00pm, Jones had heard the click of a door. He was almost sure that this must have been the front door and assumed that it meant someone had just left the premises.

By now, the police knew that the dead woman was not, in fact, Mrs Armstrong. Items found in her luggage showed that she was actually seventeen-year-old Peggy Irene Violet Pentecost. She preferred to be known by her second name, and lived at 148 Elm Grove, Brighton, with her parents.

The Brighton police were then contacted and they spoke to Edwin Pentecost, Irene's father. He was able to suggest that the man who had been with Irene in the London hotel was thirty-eight-year-old Harry Armstrong, a houseman at the Downs School, Seaford. Further, Edwin was able to supply an address for Armstrong: 12 Hindover Road, also in Seaford.

That address was the next port of call and it was there that Armstrong's landlady, Florence May Passingham, was able to confirm that Armstrong had lodged with her since October 1937. She had last seen her lodger at around 6.15pm on 30 December when he told her that he was going to spend the weekend with Irene, in Brighton. As if extra confirmation were needed, Florence was also able to positively identify one of the suitcases from the hotel, and a pair of men's pyjamas, as belonging to Armstrong.

Officers now returned to Elm Grove to check up on the story that Armstrong had planned to spend the weekend in Brighton. Edwin Pentecost confirmed that, despite the age difference, he and his wife had approved of the relationship between Armstrong and their daughter. It had indeed been their intention to spend that weekend at Elm Grove, and Armstrong arrived there on the evening of 30 December and slept at their house that night.

Early the next morning, Armstrong announced that he and

Irene were now engaged but this good news was tempered somewhat when Edwin had a minor argument with his daughter over some other matter. By 6.30pm, Irene announced that she and Armstrong were going away for the rest of the weekend. That had been the last time Edwin saw either of them.

By speaking to Richard Jones at the hotel, and also Mr and Mrs Pentecost and Florence Passingham, the police were able to put together an excellent description of Harry Armstrong. This was circulated to police stations throughout London but in the event, in hardly proved necessary for, unbeknown to Inspector Fury, Armstrong was already in custody.

At 3.30pm on 2 January, Sergeant Richard Ford had been on duty in Baker Street when he saw a man who was apparently much the worse for drink. The man was swearing loudly and generally making a nuisance of himself to people as they passed by. Sergeant Ford spoke to the man and asked him for his name. The man identified himself as Thomas King of Bydown, Seaford but was still arrested for abusive behaviour and escorted to the Albany Street Police Station. Once there, King was searched and a postcard found in his pocket. Addressed to Mrs Pentecost of 148 Elm Grove, Brighton, the card read: 'Dear Mother, This is the best way out. Love. Harry'. This card, and the description circulated by Inspector Fury left no doubt; Thomas King was none other than Harry Armstrong.

At 9.00pm that evening, Inspector Fury interviewed Armstrong for the first time and informed him that he was being detained on suspicion of causing the death of Irene Pentecost. Armstrong would only reply: 'I am saying nothing. I was not the last person with her. I can prove I was not in York Road last night after ten o'clock. I can prove where I was, but I am not going to say where I was now. I am saying nothing. I neither admit nor deny anything. I will tell the magistrate in the morning.' Armstrong was then taken to Kennington Road Police Station where Inspector Fury formally charged him with murder.

The trial was originally due to start on 13 February but on that date, an application was made for Armstrong to undergo a medical examination. Consequently, the trial was postponed and only finally opened on 1 March at the Old Bailey, before Mister Justice Humphreys. Throughout the two days of the proceedings, Armstrong was defended by Mr J F Eastwood. The case for the Crown lay in the hands of Mr L I Byrne.

One of the first witnesses was the dead girl's father, Edwin Pentecost. He explained that Irene had once worked as a maid at a school in Seaford and that was how she had first met Armstrong. She had first brought Armstrong to her parent's house in Brighton in June 1938 and they appeared to be very much in love with each other.

Armstrong and Irene had been in London from the evening of 31 December until she was discovered lying dead in the hotel on 2 January. What had the couple been doing during that stay? Part of the answer was supplied by James Norris, an old friend of Irene's.

Though James now lived at 19 Brock Road, Walthamstow, he had once lived in Brighton and had kept in touch with Irene. At around 3.00pm on 1 January, Irene had called at his home, bringing Armstrong with her and introducing him as her fiancé. The couple stayed with James and his wife until about 5.30pm and during the time they were there they behaved very affectionately towards each other. At one stage, Irene had even sat upon Armstrong's knee.

Chief Inspector Frederick Cherrill was in charge of the fingerprint department of New Scotland Yard and he had made an examination of the hotel room in York Road. He had carefully examined the sherry bottle and the tumbler found inside the room and found that both carried prints. One print, found on the bottle, matched Armstrong's right middle finger and another on the tumbler matched his left thumb. One other print was found on the bottle and this belonged to neither Armstrong or Irene. It was obscured somewhat by a partial print from Armstrong so was assumed to have been already on the bottle when it was purchased.

Irene's body had been examined by Dr Keith Simpson and he testified that there was some bruising to Irene's lips, probably caused when the blanket was stuffed into her mouth. Beneath this

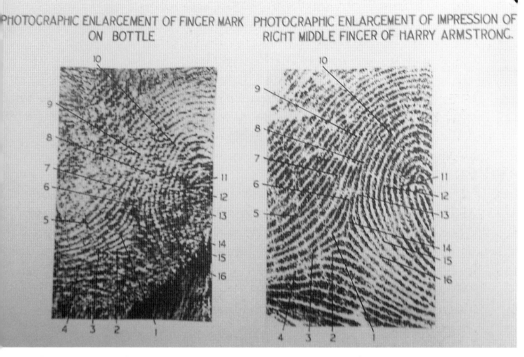

PHOTOGRAPHIC ENLARGEMENT OF FINGER MARK ON BOTTLE

PHOTOGRAPHIC ENLARGEMENT OF IMPRESSION OF RIGHT MIDDLE FINGER OF HARRY ARMSTRONG.

Comparisons of the fingerprint found on the sherry bottle in room 6, with the fingerprint of the accused, Harry Armstrong. The National Archives

white coverlet, Simpson had found a man's hankerchief also stuffed into Irene's mouth and this had been crammed in very tightly. Simpson found marks on Irene's throat which were consistent with the thumb and forefingers of a man's left hand. This was a rather difficult point for the prosecution since Armstrong was known to be right-handed. In addition, Simpson had found bruising around the vagina which was consistent with recent rough intercourse, possibly at or around the time of death. Simpson was also able to say that the cause of death had been asphyxia, due to the combined effects of strangulation and suffocation.

The time of death would prove to be very important. Dr Simpson had made his initial examination at noon on 2 January and he put the time of death at some thirteen hours previously; that is around 11.00pm on 1 January, which matched precisely with the noise of the front door closing, heard by Richard Jones.

The inference was obvious; Armstrong had killed Irene at 11.00pm or slightly before, and left the hotel immediately afterwards. There was, however, a major problem with that scenario. Harry Armstrong had a cast iron alibi for 11.00pm.

Rose Kirby lived in St George's Road, London and she told the court that she had met Armstrong in a café in Westminster Bridge Road just after 10.00pm. She and Armstrong had then spent the entire night together in another hotel. At the time Irene Pentecost was being assaulted and murdered, Harry Armstrong was with Rose Kirby.

Having heard Rose's testimony, the prosecution had to cast doubts on the time of death. Dr Simpson was recalled to the stand and asked if it were possible that Irene had died earlier that the 11.00pm he had originally said. Simpson now agreed that Irene could have died between 9.30pm and 11.00pm after all and so Armstrong's alibi was destroyed.

Armstrong's defence team was certainly thorough and left nothing to chance in the defence of their client. Some days before the trial they had told two solicitor's clerks to enter the hotel at 22 York Road, after midnight, and leave again after a few minutes. The purpose of this experiment was to see if the manager, Richard Jones, could after all hear the front door opening and closing. He had to admit that he heard nothing of the comings and goings of the two clerks, thus showing that anyone could have entered and left at any time on the fateful night, without necessarily having been heard.

Armstrong stepped into the witness box to give his own version of events. He claimed that he had left the hotel at 9.30pm, leaving Irene asleep in the bed. He walked to Westminster Bridge Road and entered a café there, where he met Rose Kirby and some of her friends, at around 10.00pm. Later still, he and Rose booked into a hotel in Paddington where they spent the night together. He left that hotel at 9.30am the next morning.

Armstrong said that after leaving Rose he was very ashamed at what he had done; being unfaithful to Irene, so he went to a public house and had a number of drinks. He was intending to return to Irene at the hotel, once he had fortified his courage with alcohol, and make his peace with her, but before he could he was arrested by the police. As for the postcard found on his person, that was meant as an explanation for them having to leave Elm Grove that weekend after Irene had argued with her father.

One of the final witnesses was Dr Hugh Grierson, the medical officer at Brixton prison where Armstrong had been held. He told the court that he had observed no signs of mental disorder in the prisoner but there were indications that he had an uneven, quick temper. Under cross-examination, however, Dr Grierson had to confirm that there was evidence of mental instability within Armstrong's family. A younger sister, who had been feeble minded, had died at the age of eleven. An elder brother had committed suicide, as had a great uncle. Yet another uncle had died in an asylum. As for Armstrong himself, he had very bad eyesight being almost blind in his left eye and having only slightly better vision in the right. He had, during his lifetime, suffered three periods of memory loss, the last one being in 1931. Finally, in 1935, he had been charged with attempting to take his own life by means of an overdose of aspirin tablets.

In his summation for the defence, Mr Eastwood made great store of the way the prosecution had recalled a witness specifically to destroy Armstrong's alibi by altering his professional and expert opinion as to the time of death. Such a move was described as unprecedented in an English courtroom and should, of itself, lead to a verdict of not guilty.

In the event, such arguments did not sway the jury. They retired to consider their verdict at 3.33pm and at 4.10pm, returned to announce that Armstrong was guilty as charged. Asked if he had anything to say before the sentence of death was passed, Armstrong turned to the jury and said: 'Ladies and gentlemen. I appreciate everything you have done. No doubt you have had a very difficult task. In spite of your verdict, I am not guilty of the murder of Irene Pentecost.'

No appeal was entered. Armstrong's defence team decided instead to rely on a public petition for a reprieve on medical grounds. The petition was well supported but despite this, the Home Secretary announced that he had advised His Majesty that

Harry Armstrong. This picture was taken from a newspaper report after he had been sentenced to death. Author's collection

there were no grounds for such a reprieve and the death sentence would be carried out.

On Tuesday 21 March 1939, Harry Armstrong was hanged at Wandsworth prison by Thomas Phillips and Albert Pierrepoint.

At his trial, Armstrong's defence had concentrated on the fact that he had an alibi for the estimated time of death. It was, perhaps, a mistake to do so and in reality a better approach might have been to concentrate on their client's mental problems, for Harry Armstrong had been in trouble with the police before.

Many of these encounters with the law were for relatively minor offences. Thus, for example, Armstrong had served time in prison for housebreaking, shopbreaking and larceny. Of more import, though, was his very first sentence.

In 1925, Armstrong was working at an establishment known as Dorney House. Also working there was a young woman named Mabel Brown and the two started walking out together. In due course, Mabel announced that she was pregnant and that Armstrong was the father. On 20 March, the couple argued about this, on the golf links at Sunningdale, and this ended when Armstrong battered Mabel about the head and plunged a knife into her throat.

Mabel was rushed to Windsor Hospital and was not expected to survive. Armstrong was arrested and charged with attempted murder. Eventually, however, Mabel did recover and the charge against her assailant was reduced to unlawful wounding. On 30 June 1925, Armstrong appeared at the Surrey Assizes where he was sentenced to fifteen months by Mister Justice Talbot.

At first, it may be suggested that, if anything, this reinforces the idea of Armstrong's guilt for the murder of Irene Pentecost all the more certain but we also need to consider his background. Armstrong was the fourth of seven children and at the time of his birth his mother suffered from syphilis, meaning that Armstrong acquired it in its hereditary form. As a child he was always slow and was always unable to control himself. He was very slow at school and could hardly read and write.

At his trial for murder, Armstrong's defence team really skated over the suggestion that Armstrong was not of average mentality. He was, of course, examined by a doctor, one Ellis Stungo, who stated that Armstrong did not know the name of the present King, or the Prime Minister. Asked to name a member of the Cabinet, he replied Lloyd George. Dr Stungo finally concluded that Armstrong was a high-grade mental defective and could not be considered responsible for his actions.

It is probable that Harry Armstrong did kill Irene Pentecost because he believed she was seeing another man. However, that did not make him responsible for his actions. By concentrating on the defence of alibi, his defence team failed to capitalise on his obvious mental instability, which should, in turn, have raised doubts about his culpability.

That alone is reasonable doubt and Armstrong should have had the benefit of that doubt and, consequently, a not guilty verdict, by reason of insanity.

Chapter 7

Timothy John Evans
1950

At 3.10pm on Wednesday 30 November 1949, a rather nervous looking young man walked into Merthyr Tydfil police station, approached the officer on duty and asked if he might possibly speak to either a sergeant, or better still, an inspector.

The constable behind the desk, Gwynfryn Howell Evans couldn't really be bothered with such nonsense and told the man that there was no other officer available. If he had something he wished to say, or report, then he had better do it to Constable Evans himself. At that point the young man volunteered: 'I want to give myself up. I have disposed of my wife.'

Not surprisingly, Constable Evans now changed his mind and decided that it might be a good idea if a senior officer spoke to this man. As a matter of duty, Constable Evans first cautioned the man but he seemed to ignore this and continued: 'I put her down the drain.' Constable Evans asked the man if he knew that what he was saying was a very serious matter and the man replied: 'Yes, I know what I am saying. I cannot sleep and I want to get it off my chest.' Immediately he was taken through to the CID office where he was interviewed by Detective Sergeant Gough, who carefully took down the statement the man now made.

The nervous young man who had walked into the police station was twenty-five-year-old Timothy John Evans, a native of Merthyr, who had until very recently been living in London in a top-floor flat at 10 Rillington Place, Notting Hill, with his wife Beryl and their baby daughter, Geraldine. According to Evans' statement, at the beginning of October, Beryl had told him that she was expecting another child and by then, was approximately three months pregnant. Evans had, after some discussion, said that one more mouth to feed wouldn't make much difference to their circumstances but Beryl had had a different opinion. She didn't want this second child and said she wanted to get rid of it. Evans had objected to this, concerned that the procedure might make Beryl ill but she was adamant. Soon afterwards, she bought herself a syringe and began trying to abort herself. This failed but it did nothing to damped Beryl's determination. She told her husband that she had bought some tablets, which she believed would do the trick.

On the morning of Sunday 6 November, Beryl had complained that it was obvious that the tablets weren't working either. So desperate was she becoming now that she told Evans that if she couldn't find a way to get rid of the baby, she would do away with herself. Evans tried to calm his wife down but the next morning, Monday 7 November, as he left to go to work, Beryl told him that she was going to see a woman who would be able to help her.

By coincidence, it was that same day, 7 November, that Evans pulled into a transport café somewhere between Ipswich and Colchester. He fell into conversation with another driver and told him about the problems he was having at home. The driver told Evans to wait for a few minutes, and then left the café. When he returned, he was carrying a small bottle, wrapped in brown paper. He handed this to Evans and said: 'Tell your wife to take it first thing in the morning before she has any tea, and then to lay down on the bed for a couple of hours and that should do the job.'

Evans took the bottle and put it into his coat pocket, forgetting all about it. When he got home that night, he hung his coat up as usual. Soon afterwards, Beryl asked him for a cigarette and, going through his coat pockets, found the bottle. Evans told her about the encounter with the man in the roadside café and explained to Beryl what he had said she needed to do.

The next morning, Tuesday 8 November, Evans went to work as usual but first warned Beryl that she shouldn't take the stuff from the bottle. That evening, however, when he returned home, he found baby Geraldine crying in her cot and his wife lying dead on the bed.

Evans panicked and had no idea what he could do now. Rather than let the authorities know what had happened he decided to conceal the body himself. Having first fed a rather hungry Geraldine and put her back to bed, he had waited until some time between 1.00am and 2.00am the next morning when he had carried Beryl downstairs and out of the house. In the street outside was a drain. Evans lifted the cover, pushed Beryl head-first into the drain and then replaced the cover.

Later that same day, having got someone to look after Geraldine, Evans went into work as normal. He told his employer that he wished to leave as he had found a better position and, later still, sold all his furniture, for which he received £40. The items were not actually collected until Monday 14 November after which Evans caught the 12.55pm train from Paddington to Merthyr where he stayed with a relative.

The first thing for the police to do, was to check the story for themselves. Whilst Evans was held in custody, the Welsh police sent a message to their colleagues in London and asked them to check the drain in Rillington Place. That afternoon, officers from Notting Hill police station found the drain exactly where Evans had said it would be. The problem was that it took three burly officers to lift the cover, something that Evans had said he had done alone. Further, there was no sign of a body in the cavity beneath. Those details were now passed back to Merthyr.

It was 9.00pm on 30 November by the time the officers in Wales told Evans that nothing had been found in the drain. They also informed him that his story was obviously untrue since there was no way he could have lifted the cover unaided. Evans was asked if he wished to make a new statement, and he said that he would.

The second statement Evans made took some three hours to dictate and take down. It began by repeating the story of the man in the roadside café, the gift of the bottle but now went on to claim that the real killer of his wife had been another tenant at Rillington Place, the occupant of the ground-floor flat, one John Reginald Halliday Christie.

According to this second statement, sometime around 1 November, or around a week before his wife had died, he had been approached by Mr Christie who had said that he knew about the tablets Beryl was taking and had deduced why she was taking them.

He went on to say that they were being silly and, if they had come to him in the first place, he would have been able to help them.

Evans had asked Christie what he knew about medicine and Christie had told him that he had trained as a doctor before the war. He showed Evans some medical textbooks. This did little to help, however, as Evans could not read but Christie continued with his story and added, as a warning, that the 'stuff' he used to carry out the operation, would kill one person in every ten that took it. In short, there was a ten percent chance that Beryl would die. Evans told Christie that he wasn't interested.

Back inside his own flat, Beryl began applying new pressure for an abortion. Apparently, Mr Christie had already spoken to her on the matter and, despite the risks, Beryl was totally in favour of it. The couple argued and Beryl ended by saying that it was her business and she would do as she pleased.

When Evans came home from work on Monday 7 November, Beryl told him that she had seen Mr Christie and all the arrangements had been made. The operation was to take place the following morning, 8 November. Evans did not rise to the bait and refused to discuss the matter any more.

The next morning, as Evans as leaving for work, Beryl told him to call in on Mr Christie and tell him that everything was all right. Again seeking to avoid confrontation, Evans had done as she asked. That night, when he arrived home from work, he was met by Christie, who told him to go upstairs to his flat and he would speak to him there. Once inside Evans' kitchen, Christie told him: 'It's bad news. It didn't work.' He went on to explain that Beryl had died.

Beryl's body lay on the bed, covered with an eiderdown. According to Evan's statement, when he pulled the eiderdown back, he saw that she had been bleeding from the mouth, the nose, and the 'bottom part' meaning her vagina.

Christie had then lit the fire for Evans and told him to feed the baby. Evans did so and at 9.00pm, Christie returned and gave him some further information. Beryl had died at around 3.00pm from what Christie called septic poisoning. They discussed the matter and decided to hide the body in the middle flat. This belonged to Mr Kitchener, but at the time he was in hospital so his flat was empty.

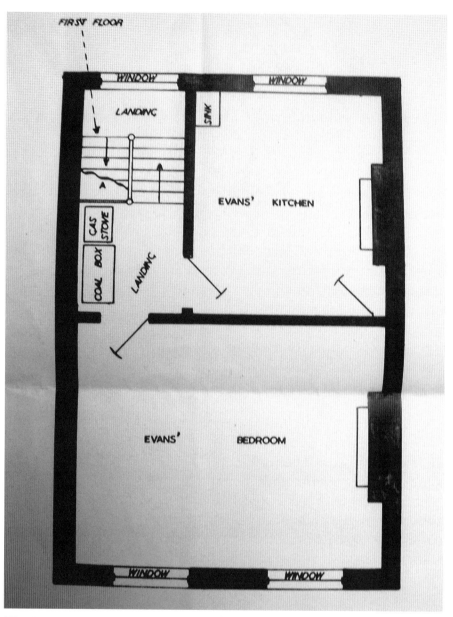

The layout of Timothy Evans' top floor flat at 10 Rillington Place. The National Archives

After further discussion, Christie said that they should dispose of the body down the drain outside and also said that he would find someone to take care of Geraldine. The very next morning, Christie told Evans that he knew of a couple in East Acton, who would take the baby for him. That same night, Wednesday 9 November, Christie told Evans that he had indeed put Beryl's body down the drain. As for Geraldine, the couple had called and she was now being well looked after.

Later still on 9 November, Evans had gone to his mother's house at 11 St Mark's Road and told her that Beryl and Geraldine had gone for a short break to Brighton. Beryl had originally come from Brighton, and had family and friends there, so this story was not suspicious. The rest of the statement was much the same as Evans' first. He had sold his furniture, travelled up to Merthyr and gone to his aunt's house at 93 Mount Pleasant.

Almost as soon as this second statement had been written out and signed, Evans began to add further, sometimes contradictory elements. He admitted that Christie had not moved the body by himself but claimed that he had heard him labouring on the stairs and had gone out to help him. This did still not explain why Beryl's body had not been found, when the drain cover had been lifted by the police. In order for this case to progress and the truth, finally, be told, Beryl's body had to be found. Once again, the Welsh police contacted their London based counterparts. A number of officers, including Detective Inspector James Neil Black, and Chief Inspector George Jennings, now returned to 10 Rillington Place to organise and supervise a second search.

On their first visit to Rillington Place, the search had been somewhat cursory and had concentrated on the drain in the street outside. Now, on this second search, although officers were much more thorough, one area was still overlooked. In the back garden was a wash-house and Chief Inspector Jennings asked one of his officers if this had been checked. He was told that it had been. In fact, some officers believed that it belonged to the house next door so in fact, it was still not examined.

On 1 December, Evans was questioned again, having been told that no trace of his wife had yet been found. Now he volunteered yet more information, admitting that he had been back to London on 21 November and returned to Merthyr two days later, on 23 November.

It seemed that the only way to take this case forward was for the London police to take charge of the prisoner and question him. For that reason, on Friday 2 December, Inspector Black and

The wash house in the yard of 10 Rillington Place, where the two bodies were eventually found. The National Archives

Detective Sergeant Corfield travelled to Wales to escort Evans back to London. That same day, at 11.50am, officers including Detective Superintendent Barratt and Chief Inspector Jennings returned to Rillington Place to organise a third search. It was during this search that, finally, the wash-house was examined.

Inside that wash-house, hidden underneath a sink, behind some planks of wood, was a large package, wrapped in a green table cloth and a blanket and tied, very tightly, with a sash-cord. It was Chief Inspector Jennings who removed the timber and pulled the

A view of the inside of the wash house. The two bodies are hidden behind the wood on the left hand side of the picture. The National Archives

package out. The sash-cord was cut and the package opened. Inside lay the doubled-over body of a woman with her head forced down towards her feet. Further, behind the door of the wash-house was the body of a baby girl, dressed in a pink woollen coat, a flannelette frock, white vest and white plastic pants. Beryl and Geraldine Evans had finally been found.

At 9.35pm, Evans and his escort arrived at Paddington station from where he was taken to Notting Hill police station. There he was shown the rope and wrapping that had contained the bodies of his wife and daughter. He was cautioned again and made a third statement, which was taken down in writing. This began: 'She was incurring one debt after another and I could not stand it any longer, so I strangled her with a piece of rope and took her down to the flat below the same night, whilst the old man was in hospital.

The body of Beryl Evans, before the wood as removed. The National Archives

'I waited till the Christies downstairs had gone to bed, then took her to the wash-house after midnight. That was on the Tuesday 8 November. On Thursday evening, after I came home from work, I strangled my baby in our bedroom with my tie and later that night I took her down to the wash-house after the Christies had gone to bed.

Evans signed that third statement and then said: 'It is a great relief to get it off my chest. I feel better already. I can tell you the cause that led up to it.' He was then asked if he wished to make a further statement, which he did. This fourth and final statement was the longest of all and as not completed until 11.15pm.

Beryl Evans, after the wood masking her body had been removed
The National Archives

In this fourth statement, Evans began by outlining his work history and then referring to Beryl running up debts. The rent had fallen into arrears and they argued about this, at one stage he told her that if she didn't improve, he would leave her. Beryl told him that as far as she was concerned, he could leave at any time he wished. They argued constantly during early November until, on the night of 8 November, during yet another row, he hit her across the face. She hit him back and, in a fit of temper, he grabbed a piece of rope and strangled her.

It had been some time before 10.00pm when he carried Beryl's body down to the vacant middle-floor flat before going back to his own and feeding Geraldine. He then put the baby to bed and waited for the rest of the house to fall quiet. He went down to Mr Kitchener's flat, wrapped Beryl's body in the table cloth and blanket and then took her out the back door and into the wash-house.

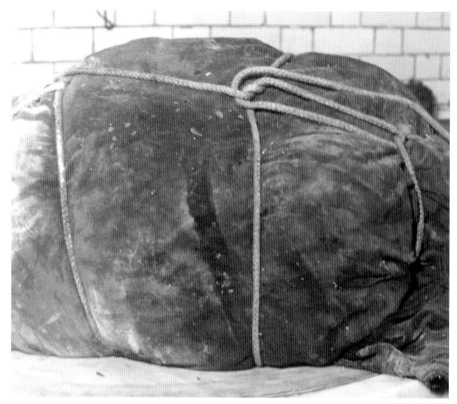

The parcel containing Beryl Evans' body. The National Archives

The next day, he fed Geraldine and then went to work as usual. He did the same thing on Thursday 10 November, but when he got home from work he strangled Geraldine too and put her body in the wash-house.

After making this last statement, Evans was taken back to the cells and allowed to rest for the night. The next morning, 3 December, he was charged with the murder of his wife, Beryl Susanna Evans. Finally, on 15 December, he was charged with the murder of his daughter, Geraldine.

No matter how many murders a man is accused of, it is customary in British courts, to proceed on just one case. So it was that when Timothy John Evans appeared at the Old Bailey, on 11 January 1950, before Mister Justice Lewis, he faced just one charge, that of the murder of his baby daughter. The trial was to last for three days, during which Evans was defended by Mr Malcolm Morris. The case for the prosecution was led by Mr Christmas Humphreys, who was assisted by Mr Henry Elam.

After the various police officers had given their evidence, the prosecution called Professor Donald Teare, the pathologist who had performed the post-mortems on both bodies. Although the charge Evans faced was the murder of his daughter, evidence would also be given on Professor Teare's findings on Beryl Evans.

According to the professor, Beryl had died from asphyxia caused by strangulation by some form of ligature. There had been deep bruising in the muscles of the right side of the voice box and small haemorrhages had been detected in the lungs and also on the chin.

Beryl had been approximately four months pregnant when she died but there was no evidence of any attempt at abortion. There was, however, a bruise on the inner left thigh, some four inches

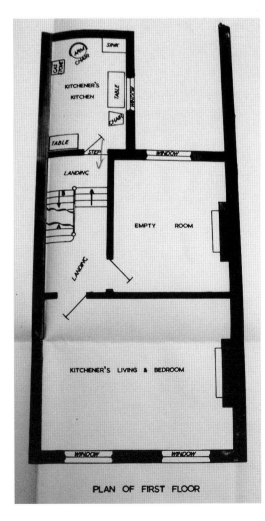

The layout of Mr Kitchener's flat on the first floor at 10 Rillington Place. The National Archives

above the knee and another on the left calf just below the knee. These bruises, along with others on the lower back wall of the vagina were consistent with rough or forced sexual intercourse.

Turning to the baby, it was clear that the cause of death was strangulation by ligature. The tie was still fastened very tightly around her throat when her body was discovered. This tie had been cut off and shown to Evans who had identified it as his. Baby Geraldine bore no other signs of injury.

The next two witnesses were John Christie and his wife. The first of these, Mr Christie, began by confirming that Mr Kitchener from the middle flat had been taken into hospital in early November 1949.

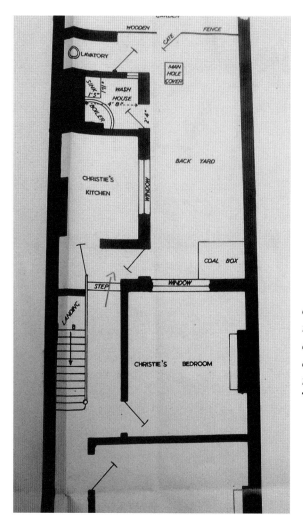

The layout of Christie's flat on the ground floor. Note the only lavatory for the entire house, at the far side of the wash house where the two bodies were discovered. The National Archives

Continuing his evidence, Christie said that the last time he had seen Beryl Evans alive was around lunch-time on 8 November. She was leaving the house at the time, pushing Geraldine in her pram. Later that day, Christie had gone to the doctor's and by the time he returned to Rillington Place, it was around 7.00pm. He and his wife retired for bed at their usual time but at approximately midnight they were woken by a loud bang. This bang was followed by another sound, as if someone were moving something heavy.

The following evening, Wednesday 9 November, he had seen Evans between 10.30pm and 11.00pm. Christie's wife, Ethel, was there and she asked Evans how his wife and baby were and he replied that they had gone away to Bristol for a few days.

At around 7.00pm on Thursday 10 November, Evans knocked on Christie's door and told him that he had argued with his employer and packed his job in. He went on to say that he too was going to go to Bristol as there might be more chance of finding a job there.

Further developments took place on Friday 11 November when Evans told Christie that he had arranged to sell all his furniture and someone would be calling for it. On the following Monday, Christie saw a van arrive and take all the furniture away. Soon afterwards, Evans showed him a roll of banknotes, money he said he had got from the sale and, soon after this, Christie saw Evans leave, carrying a large suitcase with him.

That was the last time Christie saw Evans until Wednesday 23 November when he called again between 5.30pm and 5.45pm. Evans said he had been to Bristol and from there had moved on to Cardiff, Birmingham, Coventry and then back to Cardiff but hadn't found any work. He also added that Beryl had walked out on him, taking the baby with her.

Much of this evidence was confirmed by Ethel Christie. She too had been woken by the loud bang at midnight on 8 November. She was also able to confirm most of the other conversations that her husband had told the court about. Ethel also referred to the wash-house where the bodies had been discovered, stating that it had not been used for some time, the tenants of the house only ever using the tap there for water.

The next witness was Violet Gwendoline Lynch, who was Evans' aunt and lived in Merthyr Tydfil. She confirmed that her nephew had come to stay with her on 15 November, telling her that his wife and child were in Brighton. Evans stayed with her until 23 November when he said he was going back to London. Two days later he was back and telling her that Beryl had walked out of their flat in Rillington Place but left Geraldine behind. He had given the baby to some people who lived in Newport, so that she would be looked after properly.

Violet Lynch found this all very hard to believe so she wrote to Beryl's mother in London, asking her if she knew what was going on. On 30 November she received a reply in which Beryl's mother said she hadn't seen or heard from her daughter in over a month. Faced with this information, Evans blew up into a temper and refused to eat his breakfast. He then left the house and, she now knew, had walked into the police station and given himself up.

After Constable Evans, the officer at Merthyr, had confirmed the details of the prisoner coming into the police station and confessing to disposing of his wife, the prosecution called Detective Inspector James Neil Black. That officer had had charge of Evans during one of his appearances at the West London Magistrates' Court on 3 December. After being remanded, Evans had said: 'There is something I meant to tell you Mr Black.'

Evans was immediately reminded that he was under caution but continued: 'After I killed my wife, I took her wedding ring from her finger and sold it to Samuel's at Merthyr for five shillings.' Unbeknown to Evans, the police had already checked the jeweller's in Merthyr and found the ring at Samuel's shop, which was situated at 119 High Street.

On the third day of the trial, 13 January, the jury retired to consider the evidence. After a short deliberation they returned to announce that Evans was guilty of the murder of his daughter. An appeal was entered, heard on 20 February, and dismissed. Just over two weeks later, on Thursday 9 March 1950, Timothy John Evans was hanged at Pentonville by Albert Pierrepoint and Syd Dernley.

That would have been the last that history heard of Timothy Evans but for further events that took place at 10 Rillington Place in 1953. In that year a new tenant found three female bodies walled into an alcove in the downstairs flat. Further investigations revealed the strangled body of Ethel Christie, buried beneath the floorboards in the front room. Finally, the remains of two more bodies were discovered in the back garden. In due course, John Reginald Halliday Christie was arrested and charged with murder. Found guilty, he was executed at Pentonville, on 13 July 1953, on the same gallows that had claimed Evans' life.

Christie had originally been charged with the six murders detailed above but, during one of his interviews with the police he also claimed to have murdered Beryl Evans, though he persisted in denying that he had anything to do with the death of baby Geraldine.

Disquiet over the conviction of Timothy Evans grew, culminating in a book written by Ludovic Kennedy: *10 Rillington Place* (London, Victor Gollancz Ltd, 1961). A subsequent inquiry decided that whilst Evans had possibly murdered his wife after all, there was a strong probability that he was not guilty of the charge that had condemned him to hang; the murder of Geraldine. Eventually, on 18 October 1966, a Royal pardon was granted. However, despite this, it is actually very likely that Evans was guilty of the murder of both Beryl and Geraldine. In order to examine this suggestion further, we need to look at certain aspects of both cases.

It is true that Christie was a strangler and that he used a ligature to despatch his victims. However, in every case, except the murder of his own wife, Christie's method was a contraption which bubbled household gas through a solution of Friar's Balsam. This would render his victim either unconscious or, at the very least, unable to resist and Christie would then strangle them during intercourse. Every single one of the three bodies found in the alcove of his kitchen showed signs of carbon monoxide poisoning and each body contained spermatozoa.

There can be little doubt that at the time of Beryl's post-mortem, the obvious signs of carbon monoxide poisoning would have shown up had they been present. Once Christie's infamy had come to light, Beryl's body was exhumed and still no signs of such poisoning were detected. Added to this, no traces of spermatozoa were found in Beryl's body. If Christie had murdered Beryl, then his motive had to be, as with all the others, a sexual assault and subsequent gratification. If Beryl Evans had died at Christie's hands, then his sperm would have been found in her body at that first post-mortem.

There are other factors too. Although Christie was a tall man, he was weak and ineffectual and would shy away from any physical confrontation. Evans, on the other hand, had a violent temper and often threatened his wife. The police pictures of Beryl's body clearly show that she had been the victim of a brutal physical assault. This was hardly Christie's style but it fitted Evans' emotional make-up.

Then there is also the evidence of time. Beryl Evans was seen alive, on Tuesday 8 November, by Ethel Christie. It was around lunch time and Beryl left the house, pushing the baby in her pram. She was not seen returning and at the time, there were builders in the house, working on the wash-house in the back garden. That evening, at 5.30pm, the Christies went out to the cinema. By his own statement, Evans had only returned to the flat at 6.30pm, one hour after the Christies had left. If Christie were Beryl's murderer then he had, presumably, left her body upstairs for her husband to find. Surely Evans would immediately have reported this find to the police.

Next we have the post-mortem evidence of bruising. The marks on Beryl's legs were suggestive of forced intercourse and had, in the opinion of the pathologist, been caused some days before her death. If this sexual assault were at Christie's hands then Beryl would have reported the matter. If it were at Evans' hands, then it is suggestive of marital rape and again shows him as a violent individual.

Then we have the evidence of the loud bang or bump, heard by both the Christies at around midnight on 8 November. Whilst it is true that if Christie were Beryl's killer then he might well invent that statement to incriminate Evans, however, Ethel Christie also heard that noise. She would have been highly unlikely to lie to protect her husband. In fact, she had already left Christie some years before after he had been jailed for theft. Surely she would have been unlikely to cover for him and put an innocent man's neck into the noose. Ethel Christie heard that bump which was almost certainly the sound of Evans moving his wife's body to the middle flat.

If then, we conclude that it is more likely that Evans did indeed kill his wife, then it follows that he was responsible for his daughter's death too. If Christie didn't kill Beryl, then he had no reason to kill the child. In short, Timothy Evans was guilty of killing both his wife and his daughter.

Even if this is true, and Evans was a double murderer, there are still grounds for suggesting that he should not have hanged and so there was indeed a miscarriage of justice. A medical examination after his arrest showed that Evans had an IQ of just 65 and he was diagnosed as an inadequate psychopath with schizoid traits. He had severe mental problems and on medical grounds alone, he should not have hanged.

Taking all into account, although probably given for the wrong reasons, Timothy Evans, it can be argued, deserved that posthumous pardon. If so, then he may be said to be the only person to receive a pardon for a murder he actually committed.

Chapter 8

Derek William Bentley
1952-53

Sunday 2 November 1952 was a perfectly normal night in the Ware household. Tomorrow was a school day so, at 9.15pm, Edith Alice Ware was tucking her nine-year-old daughter, Pearl, into bed in the front bedroom of their home at 74 Tamworth Road, Croydon. As Edith bade her daughter goodnight, she happened to glance out of the window in the direction of the warehouse on the opposite side of the road.

The side of Barlow and Parker's warehouse at Croydon. Note the drainpipes which Craig, Bentley and various police officers used to climb up to the roof. The doors at the far end lead to the stairs, which Constable Miles used. The National Archives

As she looked, Edith saw two young men stop near the gates of Barlow and Parker's warehouse. Edith thought that the two men looked rather suspicious and that feeling was almost immediately confirmed when the shorter of the two men suddenly climbed over the gate, to be followed moments later by his taller companion.

It looked like a break-in and Edith called for her husband, John, and told him what she had seen. As a public-spirited citizen, John then dashed from the house to a telephone call box just down the road, dialled 999, and reported the matter to the police. In fact, that telephone call would, once this matter had come to its terrible conclusion, earn a financial reward for John Ware from police funds.

The official police version of what happened next is well known to most students of true crime. Detective Constable Frederick Fairfax travelled to the scene in a car with Constable Norman Harrison. As they arrived another car, driven by Constable Sydney Miles, with his partner, Constable James McDonald, pulled up behind them.

Constable Fairfax climbed over the gate at the side of the warehouse and found himself in a sort of entryway. To his right was the brick wall of the warehouse itself and facing him were two doors, probably leading to the stairwell. He tried the doors but they were locked.

At about the same time, Constable McDonald joined Fairfax in the alley. It took some time for their eyes to become accustomed to the dark but when they did, the two officers saw a footprint on a window sill. The intruders, whoever they were, had climbed up onto the roof that way.

Fairfax wasted no time and climbed up a drainpipe onto the roof. An iron rail surrounded the entire roof and Fairfax ducked under this, noticing a brick stairwell to his left. There were four sizeable roof lights made from glass and iron and in the distance, a lift head. It was close to that lift head that Fairfax saw two shapes in the darkness; one tall, the other much shorter. Fairfax immediately identified himself by shouting: 'I am a police officer. Come out from behind that stack.' There was no reply.

At that point, Fairfax noticed another officer, Constable Harrison, who had, using a different route, climbed onto the roof adjoining the warehouse to the right. As Fairfax moved forward tentatively, Harrison called out to ask him if he was alright.

Once again Fairfax demanded that the two would-be burglars come out from behind the stack. This time there was an answer. A young voice called out: 'If you want us, fucking come and get us.' Fairfax replied: 'All right, I will.'

Bravely Fairfax moved forward, dashed to the right of the lift-stack and grabbed the taller of the two young men. This was nineteen-year-old Derek William Bentley. He offered no resistance whatsoever initially, as Faifax pushed him towards the stair-head, hoping that the doors there were open. Suddenly, Bentley pulled away from Fairfax and shouted: 'Let him have it Chris.'

Almost immediately the other intruder, sixteen-year-old Christopher Craig, fired a shot and Constable Harrison saw Fairfax collapse against the man he had in custody, then recover and start to struggle with him.

Constable Fairfax had been shot in the shoulder. He had recovered and grabbed Derek Bentley who had taken a few steps away from him. Fairfax struck out at Bentley, knocking him to the ground as another shot rang out. Fairfax then pulled his prisoner to a kneeling position and searched him. He found two items of interest: a knife and a knuckle-duster, both of which he confiscated. Bentley then volunteered the information: 'That's all I've got guv'nor. I haven't got a gun.'

Luckily for Fairfax, Christopher Craig now turned his attention to Constable Harrison on the other roof. Another couple of shots were fired. As Harrison slowly made his way back along the roof, away from the gunman, Fairfax finally managed to get Derek Bentley behind the safety of the brick stair-head.

It was then that Fairfax heard the sound of another officer climbing up the drainpipe he had used just minutes before. Leaving Bentley where he was, Fairfax went to the top of the pipe and saw that it was Constable James Christie McDonald who was having some considerable difficulty making the climb. Fairfax helped McDonald to the roof and told him that he had been shot in the shoulder.

Derek Bentley spoke again: 'I told the silly bugger not to use it.' Constable McDonald ignored this remark and asked Fairfax what sort of gun the other man had. Bentley replied: 'It's a .45 Colt and he's got plenty of bloody ammunition too.'

At this point the sound of running footsteps told the two officers on the roof that reinforcements were coming up the stairs and would probably soon emerge from the stairwell, presumably having either obtained the keys, or being prepared to smash the doors open. The doors did indeed burst open and the first figure out onto the roof itself was a uniformed officer. Another shot rang out and the officer went down. Constable Sydney Miles had been shot in the head.

Part of the rooftop where Craig shot Constable Miles as he burst through the door of the stair-head. Note the broken glass in the door itself. The National Archives

Yet another shot rang out and struck the doorframe. Fairfax and McDonald then dragged the still body of their fallen comrade around the staircase head. Meanwhile, the officer who had been behind Miles, Constable Harrison, seeing his fellow officer shot, threw his truncheon towards Christopher Craig. This was followed by a milk bottle, and a piece of wood but the only reply was yet another shot. Harrison then dashed out of the stairwell and joined his brother officers behind the brick wall of the stairhead.

Soon another policeman, Constable Robert Jaggs, also climbed up the drainpipe and joined the others on the roof. Jaggs poked his head out from behind the stairwell and was greeted by another shot as Craig called out: 'I am Craig. You've just given my brother twelve years. Come on you coppers, I'm only sixteen.' Seconds later he called out again: 'Come on, you brave coppers. Think of your wives.'

It was decided that Bentley had to be taken downstairs. He was pushed before the police, acting as a sort of shield and shouted out: 'Look out Chris, they're taking me down.'

'Are they hurting you Derek?' came the reply from Craig. There was no reply as Bentley was pushed inside the stairwell and shoved down the stairs. The prisoner was then taken by police car to Croydon Police Station.

Fairfax was armed by now and when he went back out onto the roof he shouted that fact to Craig. 'Come on then copper, let's have it out' was the only reply. Fairfax then dashed forward, firing as he went, with Harrison, Jaggs and McDonald behind him, whilst Craig moved to the corner of the roof. He was out of ammunition now. With a shout of: 'Give my love to…' Craig threw himself off the roof, his last words lost in the crash as he landed on an iron roof and rolled off into the garden below. Constable Lowe, who had been in that garden, threw himself on top of Craig who groaned loudly and muttered: 'I wish I was fucking dead. I hope I've killed the fucking lot.' The rooftop siege in Croydon was finally over.

Whilst Craig was taken to hospital to receive medical attention, Bentley was interviewed and made a full statement. That

The greenhouse which Craig landed in as he threw himself off the roof at the end of the siege. The National Archives

statement began: 'I have known Craig since I went to school. We were stopped by our parents going out together, but we still continued going out with each other – I mean we have not gone out together until tonight.

'I was watching television tonight (2 November 1952) and

between 8.00pm and 9.00pm, Craig called for me. My mother answered the door and I heard her say that I was out. I had been out earlier to the pictures and got home just after 7.00pm.

'A little later, Norman Parsley and Frank Fazey called. I did not answer the door or speak to them. My mother told me that they had called and I then ran out after them. I walked up the road with them to the paper shop where I saw Craig standing. We all talked together and then Norman Parsley and Frank Fazey left. Chris Craig and I then caught a bus to Croydon.

'We got out at West Croydon and then we walked down the road where the toilets are – I think it is Tamworth Road. When we came to the place where you found me, Chris looked in the window. There was a little iron gate at the side. Chris then jumped over and I followed. Chris then climbed up the drainpipe to the roof and I followed.

'Up to then Chris had not said anything. We both got out on to the flat roof at the top. Then someone in a garden on the opposite side shone a torch up towards us. Chris said: "It's a copper, hide behind here." We hid behind a shelter arrangement on the roof. We were there waiting for about ten minutes. I did not know he was going to use the gun.

'A plain-clothes man climbed up the drainpipe and on to the roof. The man said: "I am a police officer – the place is surrounded." He caught hold of me and as we walked away Chris fired. There was nobody else there at the time. The policeman and I then went round a corner by a door.

'A little later the door opened and a policeman in uniform came out. Chris fired again then and this policeman fell down. I could see that he was hurt as a lot of blood came from his forehead just above his nose. The policeman dragged him round the corner behind the brickwork entrance to the door. I remember I shouted something but forgot what it was. I could not see Chris when I shouted to him – he was behind a wall.

'I heard some more policemen behind the door and the policeman with me said: "I don't think he has many more bullets left." Chris shouted: "Oh yes I have" and he fired again. I think I heard him fire three times altogether. The policeman then pushed me down the stairs and I did not see any more.

'I knew we were going to break into the place. I did not know what we were going to get – just anything that was going. I did not have a gun and I did not know Chris had one until he shot. I now know that the policeman in uniform, that was shot, is dead.

'I should have mentioned that after the plain-clothes policeman got up the drainpipe and arrested me, another policeman in uniform followed and I heard someone call him "Mac". He was with us when the other policeman was killed.'

When he had finished making this statement, Bentley had written: 'Tis as be' which was his attempt at writing: 'This has been...'. He was unable to finish writing down the correct wording and asked a policeman to do it for him. He then signed it. In fact, Bentley signed his statement twice. The first time he mis-spelt his own name as 'Derk'. Such was the intellectual capacity of the older of the two men arrested that night.

There could be no doubt that the man who had killed Constable Miles was Christopher Craig. There could also be no

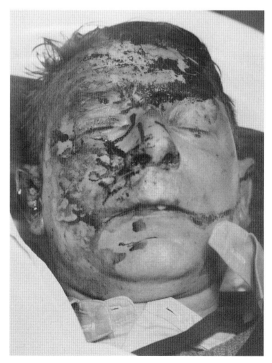

Constable Miles in the mortuary. The entry wound of the fatal bullet can clearly be seen. The National Archives

doubt that at the time of that shooting, Derek Bentley had been in police custody. However, according to those police officers who took part in the siege, Bentley had encouraged Craig to start firing with his: 'Let him have it Chris' cry. Further, despite his later statement, from the various comments he had made on the roof, Bentley had been fully aware that Craig was armed with a gun and indeed, was himself armed with a knife and a vicious looking knuckle-duster, which had a spike sticking out of the side for extra effect. All this meant that both men would stand trial for murder and, since Craig was only sixteen years old and therefore too young to hang, only Derek Bentley would face the ultimate penalty of death at the end of a rope.

The trial of Christopher Craig and Derek Bentley opened at the Old Bailey on 9 December 1952, before the Lord Chief Justice, Lord Goddard. The trial would last for three days during which the case for the Crown was led by Mr Christmas Humphreys, assisted by Mr John Stuart Bass. Bentley was defended by Mr Frank Cassels whilst Craig was represented by Mr John Parris.

The original jury consisted of ten men and two women. At the outset, Mr Parris challenged both women. They were removed and replaced by two more men, thus making an all male jury.

The first three witnesses were relatively unimportant. Chief Inspector Percy Law put into evidence photographs of the rooftop, which he had taken on 3 November, the day after the shooting. Constable Bernard Charles Beard produced some detailed plans of the rooftop, drawn to scale. Finally, Mrs Edith Ware told the court what she had seen when she looked out of the window as she put her daughter to bed on that fateful night.

The next witness was Detective Constable Fairfax, who reported his version of what had taken place on that Croydon rooftop. He was followed into the witness box by two medical gentlemen. The first of these was Dr Nicholas Jaswon, who had treated Fairfax at the Croydon Hospital. He reported a searing wound over the skin of the officer's right shoulder but was able to add that there was no fracture of the collar-bone. The bullet

Craig had fired had passed across Fairfax's skin, but had not penetrated it and had finally lodged at the back of his trousers, caught in the top of his braces.

The second medical witness was Dr David Haler, who had performed the post-mortem on Constable Miles. He told the court that Miles had been a well-built, muscular man in perfect health at the time of his death. There were two wounds in the constable's head. The first of these was at the inner side of his left eyebrow and this was the entry wound of a bullet with a large calibre. The second wound was an exit wound, slightly to the right and at the back of the head. In Dr Haler's opinion, death had been almost instantaneous.

The gun Craig had used had been examined by Lewis Charles Nickolls, the Director of the Metropolitan Police Laboratory. The barrel of this gun had been sawn down and this would have rendered the weapon highly inaccurate. The gun itself was in good working order and had a normal trigger pull. At the time of his examination, Nickolls found two bullets still inside the weapon. They had both been struck by the firing pin, but had failed to discharge.

After his arrest, Craig too had been taken to Croydon General Hospital, where he had been treated by Dr Douglas Freebody. He told the court that Craig had sustained a fracture of the dorsal spine at the level of the seventh dorsal vertebrae. There was also a fracture of the lower left forearm and a dislocation of the breastbone.

The first officer to join Fairfax on the roof had been Constable McDonald. He confirmed that he had arrived at the warehouse at 9.25pm, in the car driven by Constable Miles. A police van had arrived at the same time and Fairfax was one of the officers in that van. It had been McDonald who pointed out the footprints on the windowsill, to Fairfax, after both officers had climbed over the side gate. Fairfax had then climbed up the drainpipe but when McDonald followed, he found that he was unable to make the last six feet or so.

Hoping to find another method of entry, McDonald then began to climb back down. It was then that he heard someone, who he now knew to be Derek Bentley, shout: 'Let him have it Chris.' Shots then rang out so McDonald climbed back up and shouted for Fairfax to help him on the last part. Once on the roof, he had seen Bentley in custody.

After a few minutes, McDonald looked around the stairhead and saw Craig standing at the westerly corner of the roof. He also saw another officer, Constable Harrison, on a sloping roof near the chimney stack. Soon after this, Constable Miles was shot as he came out of the doorway.

At this point, he and Fairfax were joined by Constable Jaggs who had also climbed up the drainpipe. It was these three officers who then manhandled Bentley down the stairs.

The next witness was Constable Robert Jaggs. He testified that as he was climbing the drainpipe he heard a couple of shots fired. By the time he reached the roof, Constable Miles was already dead and his body had been dragged behind the stairhead. As Craig fired again, Jaggs heard Bentley say: 'You want to look out, he will blow your heads off.' Soon after this, Bentley was taken down and Fairfax obtained a gun and began firing back at Craig. Then Jaggs heard Craig's gun click a couple of times, before he threw himself off the roof.

Constable Norman Harrison had travelled to the scene in the van with Fairfax. As Fairfax climbed over the side gate and began to clamber up to the roof, Harrison had run around to Upper Drayton Place, where he had climbed and fence and found his way onto the roof of the factory next door at number 25 Tamworth Road. From there he managed to get onto the sloping roof of the warehouse.

Harrison saw Fairfax grab hold of Bentley on the roof, then saw him pull away soon afterwards and shout: 'Let him have it Chris.' Two shots were then fired in quick succession. Soon after this, Craig spotted Harrison and fired towards him, One bullet hit the roof somewhere behind Harrison and he then began to edge his way back. Another shot rang out and a chimney stack was hit.

Having got safely back to street level, Harrison then went inside Barlow and Parker's warehouse and up the stairs to the roof. Constable Miles was immediately in front of him and Harrison saw him kick the roof door open and rush out. A shot was fired and Constable Miles fell dead. Later still, Harrison helped his brother officers take Bentley down the stairs.

Constable Stuart Stanley Lowe had arrived at the warehouse at 9.45pm. He too climbed up the drainpipe, saw Miles lying dead, and then climbed back down again. From there he went into the garden of the house next door and saw Craig standing at the edge of the roof. Lowe heard the gun click a couple of times before Craig stood right on the edge of the roof and leapt off. It was Lowe who ran forward to grab Craig.

Bentley had been taken to Croydon Police Station in a car with Sergeant Edward Roberts and Constable Henry Thomas George Stephens. They both heard Bentley say, during that journey: 'I knew he had a gun but I didn't think he would use it. He has done one of your blokes in.'

As if there could still be any doubt as to Craig's lack of remorse, officers were then called who had had charge of him whilst he had been receiving treatment in the hospital.

Detective Sergeant Stanley Shepherd had been to see Craig at 11.00pm on the night of the shooting. At one stage Shepherd asked Craig how he felt and Criag replied: 'It's my back, it hurts.' Later he had said: 'I had six in the gun. I fired at a policeman. I had six Tommy Gun bullets.' He was immediately cautioned by Shepherd but continued: 'Is the copper dead? How about the others? We ought to have shot them all.'

Detective Chief Inspector Smith arrived at the hospital some time later to tell Craig that he would be charged with murder. To this, Craig had replied: 'He's dead is he? What about the others?'

On 5 November, Craig was being supervised by Constable Thomas Sheppard and he reported various statements the prisoner made to him that afternoon. At 2.10pm Craig had said: 'Is the policeman I shot in the shoulder still in the hospital? I know the one I shot in the head is dead.' At 3.35pm, Craig said: 'What do you get for carrying a knuckle-duster? Bentley had mine.' Finally, at 3.45pm, he had asked: 'Did you see the gun I had? It was all on the wobble so I took it to work and sawed two inches off the barrel.'

Constable Ernest Brown had charge of Craig on 6 November. At one stage Craig had said to him: 'If I hadn't cut a bit off the barrel of my gun I would probably have killed a lot more policemen. That night I was out to kill because I had so much hate inside me for what they done to my brother. I shot the policeman in the head with my .45. If it had been the .22 he might not have died.'

The final police witness was Constable John Smith who testified that when he had had charge of Craig on 3 November, he had said: 'You are coppers. Ha! The other one is dead, with a hole in his head. I'm all right. All you bastards ought to be dead.'

After Christopher Craig's father, Niven Matthews Craig, had confirmed in court that his son had been born on 19 May 1936, showing that he was too young to face the death penalty, Dr J C M Matheson, the Medical Officer of Brixton prison, was called to give evidence on Bentley's mental condition.

Dr Matheson had made a number of examinations of Bentley and he confirmed that he was the third child of a family of five. In September 1948 he had been sent to the Kirkwood Approved School at Bristol. He had remained at that establishment until 28 July 1950 and whilst there, tests had shown that he had an IQ of just sixty-six and a reading age of four and a half years. An ECG examination suggested that he suffered from petit mal. Finally, he was illiterate and had a mental age of eleven or twelve.

Both the defendants gave evidence. The first was Craig who could recall none of the statements of bravado he was supposed to have made whilst he was in hospital. More importantly, he had not heard Bentley shout: 'Let him have it Chris.' This point was taken up by the judge, the Lord Chief Justice who pointed out that three policeman had heard Bentley make the comment. Craig replied: 'I am saying I did not hear it and if they heard it, they have better ears than mine.'

When Derek Bentley gave his own testimony he said that he had not known that Craig intended to commit a burglary until he actually climbed over the fence at the warehouse. He had not known that Craig had a gun until the first shot was fired. He had not shouted: 'Let him have it Chris' and at no stage had he offered any resistance to any police officer. Finally, he had not made any reference to the type of gun Craig had, or how much ammunition he had. He couldn't tell one gun from another and knew nothing about ammunition.

In his summing up, the trial judge showed a great deal of bias. At one stage he picked up the knuckle-duster which had been found on Bentley after his arrest. Bentley had never denied that Craig had given him this weapon on the night of the shooting but he was unable to say why. To demonstrate the viciousness of the weapon, Lord Goddard placed it on his hand and smashed it down into the woodwork on the bench. He omitted, however, to make one vital point. The knuckle-duster had been found in Bentley's right hand pocket, where Craig had placed it. Bentley was left-handed.

On that final day, the jury were out considering their verdict from 11.15am until 12.30pm. When they returned, they announced that they had found both men guilty of murder, and wished to add a recommendation to mercy in the case of Bentley. Craig was then sentenced to be detained during Her Majesty's Pleasure whilst Bentley was sentenced to hang.

Bentley was originally due to hang on 31 December but an appeal was entered against his death sentence and postponed the event. The appeal was heard on 13 January and the grounds were twofold. First, that there had been misdirection by Lord Goddard in that he had summed up Bentley's defence in one sentence whilst the prosecution summary ran to four or five pages. The second argument was that the joint venture with Craig had ended at the moment of Bentley's arrest and he was, therefore, in no way responsible for the death of Constable Miles. In the event, the three judges ruled that there had been no misdirection and the joint venture had continued after Bentley's arrest. The appeal was dismissed.

Fifteen days later, on Wednesday 28 January 1953, Derek Bentley was hanged at Wandsworth prison, by Albert Pierrepoint and Harry Allen. Such was the disquiet over the event that the crowd outside tried to storm the prison gates.

Derek Bentley should not have hanged. Perhaps the first reason for suggesting this is his own personal and medical history. Born on 30 June 1933, Derek was actually a twin but his brother had died within two hours of his birth and Derek himself was not expected to survive. At the age of four, Derek was playing on a lorry when he fell off, onto his head. The boy had to be rushed to hospital where the fall brought on an epileptic seizure. The doctors told his parents that he would never be the same again.

In 1940, when Derek was seven, he and his family had been living at 136b Union Street, Southwark. On 10 September of that year, their house was bombed. Derek had to be dug free from the rubble. The family moved to 128 Hillingdon Street, but four years later, in 1944, a flying bomb fell onto that house. Medical opinion was of the belief that these events had brought on mental problems which meant that although Bentley was physically older than Craig, his mental age was actually less than that of his fellow accused.

Thus, for medical reasons alone, Derek Bentley should not have faced the death penalty, but there were other factors too. The words 'Let him have it Chris' had been heard by three police officers, and the first shot fired by Craig had followed immediately. If Bentley had ever uttered those words, which he and Craig always denied, then surely he would have argued that he meant for Craig to hand the gun over, not to shoot. It must also be remembered that a curious parallel already existed to that particular story.

On 11 July 1940, two men named Ostler and Appleby were hanged for the murder of a policeman. They had broken into a warehouse and been interrupted by the officer. Seeing that he was by himself, Appleby had shouted: 'Let him have it, he is all alone.' Ostler then shot the officer dead. At the subsequent trial, Appleby was also adjudged to be guilty of murder since he had incited Ostler to fire. The words bear a striking echo to those supposedly uttered by Derek Bentley.

Finally there is the factor of the missing policeman. Detective

Constable Fairfax always said that he had travelled to the scene in Croydon in a police van, driven by Constable Harrison. Both men omitted to mention that there had been a third policeman in that van: Constable Claude Pain. They also forgot to mention that at the same time Fairfax was climbing the drainpipe to get to the roof, Pain had obtained a ladder from one of the neighbours and reached the roof at about the same time as Fairfax, before the very first shot was fired. Pain stated that Bentley never said: 'Let him have it Chris' and instead reported that once he had been arrested, Bentley spent most of his time crying behind the stairhead after Fairfax had been shot. Pain was never called to give his testimony in any court because that testimony was tantamount to suggesting that his colleagues were either mistaken, or lying.

After Derek Bentley had been hanged, four police officers were rewarded with medals. Fairfax was awarded the George Cross, whilst Harrison and McDonald got the George Medal and Jaggs was awarded the British Empire Medal.

Bentley's family continued to maintain that their son was innocent and should not have been hanged. Every year, on the anniversary of his birthday, and also on the day he had been executed, they left flowers at the gates of Wandsworth prison, asking that they be placed on Derek's grave. Unbeknown to them, but shown in Home Office documents kept in the Public Record Office, it was always ordered that the flowers simply be destroyed.

The family also asked for permission to visit Derek's unmarked grave but the State always said no. Despite a request from the Bishop of Croydon, the prison authorities would not allow the family to see where Derek lay.

Slowly, however, the immovable State did seem to soften. In March 1966, the then Home Secretary, Roy Jenkins, gave consent to Derek's remains being exhumed for reburial by the family.

By the early 1990s, it was acknowledged by the authorities that Bentley should not have hanged, due to his mental subnormality, but it was not until 1998 that the case was finally sent back to the Court of Appeal. Here it was ruled that the trial judge had failed to adequately put the appellant's defence before the jury and also that he had failed to direct the jury to consider whether since the appellant was under arrest at the time the fatal shot was fired, the circumstances affected his responsibility for the crime.

Put into somewhat different words, they were precisely the same grounds as the original appeal in 1953. This time, however, the ruling was in Bentley's favour and the murder conviction was quashed. For Derek William Bentley, an innocent man with the mind of a twelve-year-old, it was just forty-five years too late.

Chapter 9

Colin Lattimore, Ronald Leighton and Ahmet Salih 1972

At 1.21am on the morning of Saturday 22 April 1972, the Fire Brigade was called out to a fire at 27 Doggett Road, Catford. By the time the fire officers arrived, the ground floor and basement of the house were both well alight. Nevertheless, the fire was brought under control within ten minutes and officers were sent in to determine the possible cause of the blaze. Only then did they discover, in the back bedroom upstairs, the body of a young man. This was not, however, a tragic case of someone dying in a fire, for his body had not been touched by the flames. There was a distinct mark around his neck. This was a case of murder with the fire, presumably, having been started to destroy any possible evidence. The first police officers arrived at Doggett Road at 1.45am. Some fifteen minutes later, the divisional police surgeon, Dr Angus Bain, arrived to officially pronounce the young man dead. The cause of death was given as asphyxia and an approximate time of death, calculated from the onset of rigor mortis, was that the man had been killed at some time between 8.00pm and 10.00pm the previous day, 21 April.

The usual method of determining a more accurate time of death was to take a rectal temperature. However, it was possible that the dead man was a homosexual, so no such measurement was taken for fear of destroying any evidence of recent sexual activity.

At 3.45am, the pathologist, Dr James Cameron arrived and made his own examination of the body. He slightly extended the possible time of death and put it at some time between 7.45pm and 11.45pm. Once again, Dr Cameron did not take a rectal temperature.

The murder victim was a mixed-race man, in his twenties. When he was found he was wearing fawn-coloured trousers and a long-sleeved T-shirt with an ace of clubs motif on the chest. There were obvious signs of strangulation; his lips were blue and the mark around his neck showed that some sort of cord or flex had been twisted around it.

The body was moved to Lewisham Mortuary later that same morning, where Dr Cameron performed the post-mortem. Meanwhile, a police search of the house in Doggett Road showed that the fire had certainly been started deliberately. A can of petrol had been set on fire underneath the stairs in the basement. Later still, a length of electrical flex was discovered in a dressing-table drawer in the bedroom where the body had been found. There was, however, no other evidence to connect anyone with the crime. No fingerprints had been found. However, the police had by now managed to put a name to the dead man. He was a twenty-six-year-old transvestite homosexual prostitute named Maxwell Confait, who preferred to be known as Michelle.

The police officer in charge of the investigation was Detective Superintendent Alan Jones. He began with the dead man's landlord, a West Indian man named Winston Goode.

It had been a neighbour who telephoned in details of the fire to the emergency services, but it had actually been first discovered by Mr Goode. When he was interviewed by the police, Mr Goode said that he had first met Confait a couple of years before, at about the same time as his own marriage had broken up. Goode's wife and family still lived with him in the same house but they now led completely separate lives.

Goode continued by saying that in February 1972, Confait had moved into the house at Doggett Road. The two men had become close friends but Goode swore that there had been no homosexual relationship between them. The arrangement was much simpler. Confait paid just £2.50 a week in rent but he also cooked meals for Goode whilst he was out at work.

Turning then to the night of 21 April, Goode said that he had been asleep in his room, in the basement, when he was woken by the crackling sound of the flames. He immediately dashed upstairs to warn his wife and children and also shouted up to Confait but received no reply.

The next person to be interviewed was Goode's estranged wife, and she told officers that her ex-husband had been behaving rather strangely when he woke her and the children. His eyes were wide open and he didn't seem to know precisely what he was doing. Indeed, so concerned was she that she sent a neighbour after Winston when he said he was going to telephone for the Fire Brigade. The neighbour found Winston Goode fumbling with the telephone dial and unable to complete the call so the neighbour did it for him.

Winston Goode was interviewed again and now revealed that Confait was about to leave Doggett Road. Further, Goode admitted that he had entertained feelings of jealousy when Confait had told him that he intended moving in with one of his lovers. By this stage, the police were coming to believe that this jealousy might well have been a motive for murder and all their investigations were concentrating on Winston Goode as the primary suspect. It was then that circumstances took the investigation off on a completely different tack.

The fire at Confait's home had been set in the late hours of 21 April or the early hours of 22 April. During Monday 24 April, a series of small fires were set in the Doggett Road area. A total of three small fires were set, the first of these being on a railway embankment behind Doggett Road. Another fire was set in a hut in Ladywell Fields and a third was in a derelict house in nearby Nelgarde Road. Surely it was too much for coincidence; three more malicious fires in such a small area. Perhaps these fires had some link with the murder of Maxwell Confait.

At 5.20pm on that same Monday, Constable Roy Cumming stopped a young man who seemed to be just loitering in Nelgarde Road. Asked for his name, the man said that he was eighteen-year-old Colin Lattimore and when the officer went on to question him about one of the fires set earlier that day, Lattimore readily admitted that he had been responsible.

Constable Cumming was, of course, fully aware of the Confait murder and the possibility of links with the latest fires so he now asked Lattimore about the fire in Doggett Road the previous Friday. Lattimore replied: 'I was with Ronnie. We lit it, but put it out. It was smoking when we left.'

The 'Ronnie' whom Lattimore had mentioned was fifteen-year-old Ronald Leighton who lived in Doggett Road itself. Lattimore was then escorted to Leighton's house where officers found another young man, fourteen-year-old Ahmet Salih. All three young men were then taken to Lewisham Police Station, for interview.

After a brief interview at Lewisham, the three new suspects were taken to the murder headquarters in Lee Road. There they were interviewed again, by Superintendent Jones, Detective Inspector Graham Stockwell and Detective Constable Peter Woledge.

One fact is inescapable: those interviews should not have been carried out the way they were. The youngest of the three was just fourteen and the eldest was eighteen but had a mental age of eight. Judges' Rules clearly state that when children are interviewed, as far as is practicable, a parent or guardian should be present. If that is not possible for some reason, then some person who is not a police officer and who is of the same sex as the child, should be present. All three suspects were interviewed without any such person present.

Lattimore was the first of the three to be interviewed, between 6.00pm and 6.55pm. He was followed by Leighton, between 7.00pm and 7.35pm. The last one to be spoken to was Salih and his interview lasted from 7.40pm to 8.05pm. Though it was strongly denied by the three officers involved, Lattimore and Salih both claimed that they had been struck by Constable Woledge and Lattimore said he had been pushed around. Whatever the truth is about that, the interviews ended with Lattimore and Leighton admitting to killing Confait, starting the fire at Doggett Road and starting the later three fires. Salih admitted helping to start the fires but denied any involvement in Confait's murder. Nevertheless, all three were informed that they would be charged with murder.

Almost exactly one month later, on 26 May, Salih's murder charge was dropped. He would still have to face a trial on the arson charges but for now was granted bail. Lattimore and Leighton remained in custody to face the more serious charge.

There were various appearances before the magistrates, the final one being on 2 June at Woolwich. Here the police outlined their case which showed that they believe that Leighton had done the actual strangling of Confait but it had been Lattimore who placed the flex around his throat. Later still, Salih had helped them to start the fire. The problem was that both Dr Bain and Dr Cameron had by now agreed that the murder must have taken place between 6.30pm and 10.30pm on 21 April and all three defendants had alibis for those hours. However, they had confessed to the police so it was felt that there was enough evidence to send them for trial.

What were those three alibis? Turning to Lattimore first, his defence team knew that he had been at a remedial day centre until he went home for his evening meal. After this, he went with Gary, his brother, to the Salvation Army Youth Club where they were seen by a number of witnesses. All those witnesses agreed that Lattimore was at the club until around 10.30pm.

Salih and Leighton had a common alibi. They had spent the day together at Leighton's house and they had two witnesses to this. The first was Salih's sister, Periuan and the other was a friend of hers, Deborah Ricketts. Both girls said that the boys had walked them to the bus stop outside the cinema at 9.15pm. After this, the boys had gone to a shoe shop in Sangley Road where they decided to break in to see if they could find anything to steal. They went back to Leighton's house to get a screwdriver, returned to the shop and forced their way in, taking a few pounds from the till. Later still, they decided to return to the shop and break in again. This time they were both arrested by the police. The time of that arrest was recorded at 1.30am on 22 April.

The trial of Lattimore, Leighton and Salih opened at the Old Bailey, on 1 November, before Mister Justice Chapman. The proceedings would last until 24 November, during which the case for the Crown was led by Mr Richard Du Cann. Lattimore was defended by Mr John Marriage, Leighton by Mr Cyril Solomon and Salih by Mr Brian Watling.

The defence team were certain that their clients would be acquitted. Despite the confessions, it was clear that all three were elsewhere at the time Maxwell Confait met his death, according to the combined medical expertise of Dr Bain and Dr Cameron. Unfortunately, those two medical gentlemen had now changed their minds. They both testified that taking into account the heat affecting the onset of rigor mortis they had now come to the conclusion that Confait could have died as late as 1.00am on 22 April. The three alibis were now worthless and the confessions carried much more weight. As a result, the jury were out for just three and a half hours on the final day before returning with their verdicts.

Leighton was guilty of murder, arson and burglary and was to be detained During Her Majesty's Pleasure. Lattimore was adjudged to be guilty of manslaughter and arson for which he was to be detained under the Mental Health Act, without limit of time. Salih was found guilty of arson and burglary, for which he received four years.

An appeal was entered and heard on 26 July 1973, the grounds being that the original estimate of the time of death had been correct and all three had alibis for that time period. The Appeal Court ruled that the times given at the trial were reliable, that consequently the three had no alibis and the appeal would be dismissed.

There the matter would have rested but for the efforts of George Lattimore, Colin's father. He believed firmly that a miscarriage of justice had taken place and began by making an official complaint against Constable Woledge for the alleged assault on his son. That complaint was dismissed so Mr Lattimore then began writing letters to highlight the problems with the case. He wrote to anyone he thought might be able to help and two of those letters bore fruit.

The first as to his local member of parliament, Mr Carol Johnson, who took up the case on Mr Lattimore's behalf and contacted the Home Office. They in turn told Mr Johnson that the case could only be reopened if new evidence came to light.

The second letter was to the National Council for Civil

Liberties who also took up the case and put the medical evidence into the hands of arguably one of the most famous pathologists of the day, Professor Donald Teare. In April 1974, Professor Teare submitted his report; the fire would have had no effect on the onset of rigor mortis and both Dr Bain and Dr Cameron had been correct in their first estimate. Confait had died between 6.30pm and 10.30pm on 21 April. Once again, the alibis were viable.

On 22 May, Winston Goode, the first suspect in the case, committed suicide by taking cyanide. A police inquiry was now set up to look into his death and asked to pay particular attention to any possible involvement of Mr Goode in the murder of Maxwell Confait. As part of that inquiry a secret report was commissioned from another famous pathologist, Professor Keith Simpson. His findings agreed with Professor Teare; Confait had died well before the time quoted at the trial.

That same inquiry also looked at Detective Chief Superintendent Alan Jones. Even before the Confait case, this officer had been mentioned in various reports. During the investigation into the disappearance of Mastoora Begum he had confiscated the passports of the rest of the members of her family. The Court of Appeal had declared that this action was illegal and ordered the passports returned. In another case, Jones had investigated the taking of a baby and had arrested an epileptic girl who confessed. Later it was shown that her confession was false and she had a cast-iron alibi for the time of the kidnapping.

Public opinion had also begun to swing in favour of the three prisoners. There were articles in the press and on the television news culminating in a documentary called *Time for Murder* which was transmitted on 6 November 1974. The case was re-examined by the Lord Chief Justice, Lord Widgery and finally, on 18 June 1975, the Home Secretary, Roy Jenkins, announced that he had sent the case back to the Court of Appeal.

That new appeal was heard on 6 October 1975 before Lord Justice Scarman, Lord Justice Ormond and Mr Justice Swanwick. Arthur Craven, who had given evidence at the original trial as a fire expert, was able to say that the heat in Confait's room had only been slight, thus underlining the lack of effect it would have had on the onset of rigor mortis. Inconsistencies in Winston Goode's testimony were also highlighted, and then Professor Teare entered the witness box to refute the time of death evidence given at the trial. This was strengthened further by a written report from Professor Simpson who was too ill to attend in person.

On Friday 17 October, the court gave its judgement: all three young men were exonerated from any involvement in the death of Maxwell Confait. It was also held that there was insufficient evidence on the main arson charge and the three minor fires would only ever have warranted a probationary sentence. All three were free men.

By definition, the confessions all three had made must therefore be false and in turn that meant that they must have been prompted by one or more police officers. An inquiry on that matter was held, but no blame was attached to any individual officer so no charges were ever laid against any member of the police force.

A number of suggestions were subsequently made regarding the death of Maxwell Confait. During the successful appeal, Lord Scarman himself had suggested that since there was no sign of a struggle inside Confait's flat, it was likely that he knew his killer. This led to two possibilities. Either the killer could have been Winston Goode himself or alternatively, Confait could have been accidentally killed by a lover as they engaged in some form of homoerotic strangulation.

What is certain is that mistaken medical testimony and possibly improper police behaviour had deprived three young men of more than three years of their lives.

The National Archives at Kew, where the records relating to the cases in this book, and many more, are kept. Author's collection

Index